U.S. Troops in Europe

JOHN NEWHOUSE

with Melvin Croan, Edward R. Fried, and Timothy W. Stanley

U.S. Troops in Europe

Issues, Costs, and Choices

THE BROOKINGS INSTITUTION
Washington, D.C.

Copyright © 1971 by
THE BROOKINGS INSTITUTION
1775 Massachusetts Avenue, N.W., Washington, D.C. 20036

Library of Congress Catalog Card Number 71-179325

ISBN 0-8157-6046-9 (cloth)

ISBN 0-8157-6045-0 (paper)

1 2 3 4 5 6 7 8 9

THE BROOKINGS INSTITUTION is an independent organization devoted to non-partisan research, education, and publication in economics, government, foreign policy, and the social sciences generally. Its principal purposes are to aid in the development of sound public policies and to promote public understanding of issues of national importance.

The Institution was founded on December 8, 1927, to merge the activities of the Institute for Government Research, founded in 1916, the Institute of Economics, founded in 1922, and the Robert Brookings Graduate School of Economics and Government, founded in 1924.

The general administration of the Institution is the responsibility of a Board of Trustees charged with maintaining the independence of the staff and fostering the most favorable conditions for creative research and education. The immediate direction of the policies, program, and staff of the Institution is vested in the President, assisted by an advisory committee of the officers and staff.

In publishing a study, the Institution presents it as a competent treatment of a subject worthy of public consideration. The interpretations and conclusions in such publications are those of the author or authors and do not necessarily reflect the views of the other staff members, officers, or trustees of the Brookings Institution.

Foreword

ALTHOUGH more than twenty-five years have passed since the end of the Second World War, the United States continues to maintain about one-fourth of its general purpose military forces in Western Europe. The maintenance abroad of so powerful a military presence over so long a period is unprecedented in American history.

To some, these forces are a costly anachronism reflecting the unwillingness of successive administrations to come to terms with far-reaching political and economic change in Europe. To others, they are the most economical means of meeting an important national security requirement and an essential element in the healthy political evolution of Western Europe and the maintenance of close Atlantic cooperation over a wide range of issues.

The debate on whether to keep these forces in Europe has been sharp and persistent, particularly in the Congress. In May 1971, the Senate considered at length and finally voted down a number of proposals for substantially reducing the U.S. military presence in Europe by the end of 1971. The debate promises to continue, for the underlying questions concern basic tenets of American foreign policy on which views differ sharply. Moreover, the foreign and domestic reactions to President Nixon's economic program of August 15, 1971 suggest that the issue of U.S. defense expenditures in Europe will be an important element in negotiations leading to a new economic alignment.

In this volume, John Newhouse and his collaborators explore the main questions raised in this debate. Does the changing East-West political environment in Europe mean that the military-political threat to Western Europe is significantly diminishing? Is there a militarily stable balance between NATO forces and Warsaw Pact forces in Central Europe, and how important to this balance are U.S. forces? Can Western Europe assume a greater share in NATO defense, and in what circumstances is it likely to do so? What are the budgetary and foreign exchange costs of U.S. forces in Europe, and how could they be reduced? From an analysis of these questions, the authors reach several conclusions regarding U.S. interests, choices, and future prospects.

John Newhouse, coauthor and editor of the book, was a senior fellow in the Brookings Foreign Policy Studies program during its preparation. Edward R. Fried, author of Chapter 5, is a senior fellow in Foreign Policy Studies. Chapters 2 and 3 were prepared by members of the Brookings associated staff—Melvin Croan, a professor of political science at the University of Wisconsin, and Timothy W. Stanley, currently executive vice president of the International Economic Policy Association, who took part in this study while a visiting professor of international relations at the School of Advanced International Studies of the Johns Hopkins University. Although the authors are primarily responsible for the chapters they prepared, they agree on the substance and conclusions of the book as a whole.

Henry Owen, Director of Brookings' Foreign Policy Studies program, followed the work at every stage, and his knowledge contributed precision and insight to each chapter. Francis Bator, John M. Leddy, and Richard H. Ullman made valuable comments on the entire manuscript, though of course they bear no responsibility for the final outcome.

In addition, the authors are grateful for the research assistance of present and former Brookings staff members, especially Charles P.

Shirkey, who helped with the statistics in Chapters 3 and 5; Priscilla A. Clapp, who developed background material for Chapter 2; and Arnold Kanter, who assisted with Chapters 1 and 4. Edward C. Meyer, while a federal executive fellow at Brookings, also assisted in the preparation of statistical material for Chapters 3 and 5; and Darnell M. Whitt II, a research assistant at the Johns Hopkins School of Advanced International Studies, assisted Mr. Stanley in preparing Chapter 3. Ella H. Wright edited the manuscript and Joan C. Culver prepared the index.

The work was made possible by a grant from the Anderson Foundation and by support from the Ford Foundation for the Defense Analysis Project and for other parts of the Brookings Foreign Policy Studies program.

The views expressed in this book are those of the authors and do not necessarily represent the views of the trustees, officers, or other staff members of the Brookings Institution, the Anderson Foundation, or the Ford Foundation.

KERMIT GORDON
President

August 1971
Washington, D.C.

Contents

I

Pressures against the Status Quo

AN ATTRIBUTE of great power is the responsibility of exercising it. Equally, leadership must recognize the implicit limits on national power and, in the case of a free society like the United States, the constraints arising from public and legislative opinion.

The history of the two decades following World War II was largely shaped by the adversary relationship of the great powers East and West. During this time the United States created a collective security system aimed at containing—though not reducing—Soviet power in Europe and waged war against an Asian communist state, North Korea. Public and congressional opinion throughout this period rallied behind broad commitments of American power and resources in what clearly appeared to be a defense of American—that is, Western and "free world"—interests. During the late 1960s, attitudes in America, especially in the circles most influential in shaping them, shifted from a relatively uncritical acceptance of the broad exercise of American power and resources abroad toward a tendency to challenge new commitments and to set lower limits on the resources called up by existing policies. Thus, the war with another communist state, North Vietnam, has steadily lost public (to say nothing of congressional) support and has aroused opposition, while the system on which

Western Europe's security rests and which relies on American power also faces pressure for revision.

The urge to modify the Atlantic security system, now in its third decade, is concentrated in parts of the U.S. Congress and in American university circles, but it arises from a generalized disaffection with the status quo. An important part of the debate on the security system centers around the level and composition of U.S. forces in Europe. It pits the executive branch against the legislature—notably a large number of U.S. senators, who believe that American forces in Europe could be substantially reduced without prejudice to the purposes they serve and who question whether the purposes themselves are as essential to U.S. (and Western European) security as they were in years past.

Orthodox opinion holds that the balance of power runs through Europe—that American policy under Presidents Truman, Eisenhower, Kennedy, Johnson, and Nixon has been directed primarily at avoiding a shift in the power balance away from the United States and its allies, thereby discouraging efforts of actual or potential adversaries to extend their power and influence at American expense. Thus, the executive branch tends to believe—no less now than in the past—that the burden of proof rests on those who would modify the military posture of the United States in Europe.

In sharp and notable disagreement is Senate Majority Leader Mike Mansfield of Montana, who seeks to reduce by about half the U.S. forces permanently stationed in Europe. The debate and vote in May 1971 on his proposed amendment and on the substitute versions offered by other members suggested that, even though his amendment was defeated, a majority of the Senate favors either some reduction of U.S. troop deployments in Europe or a redistribution of the financial burden they create. Senator Mansfield has said:

It is not a desirable situation for a foreign power either in Eastern Europe or Western Europe to keep somewhere in the neighborhood of a million men in these two camps, a quarter of a century after the events which initially put them there. . . . Yet the continuing presence of the one has become the principal basis for the continuing presence of the other.[1]

The skeptics, congressional and otherwise, disavow that they hold naïve assumptions about Soviet policy vis-à-vis Western Europe or that they fail to see the need for maintaining an American military presence there. Most of them recommend moving toward a smaller military presence that would reflect more accurately the degree and character of the threat to Western security posed by Soviet armed forces. As Senator Mansfield put it,

I am not now advocating, and I have not in the past advocated, that all U.S. troops be removed from Europe. Our vital interest in what transpires in Europe remains and a U.S. presence should remain. In this day and age an armed attack on Western Europe will certainly involve us almost from the outset. It is to our interest, therefore, that we are present before the outset. That need can be met, in my judgment, and should be met with a much smaller military force.[2]

American NATO Commitments

Current deployments of U.S. forces in Europe (excluding naval) amount to about 300,000 men. Of this number, the equivalent of four and one-half divisions assigned to the Seventh Army in Germany is the commitment that draws most of the congressional fire. As these units can be reinforced by four and two-thirds divisions based in the United States, nine active divisions are therefore earmarked for contingencies in the European theater. To these must be added six tactical air wings assigned to NATO and deployed in West Germany, Great Britain, and Turkey, plus another wing in Spain and other elements based in the United States. Finally, there is the Sixth Fleet, with two attack carriers on station in the Mediterranean, the carrier support, and a Marine assault task group.

Europe's defense rests also on the ultimate American commitment to counter with strategic nuclear forces 700 Soviet medium- and intermediate-range ballistic missiles deployed in western Russia, as well as 750 Badger and Blinder medium bombers capable of carrying nuclear weapons. The American weapons assigned to this role are not a part of our NATO forces or earmarked for NATO.

It can be argued that the strong American military presence in a stable, fully reconstituted, and prosperous Western Europe is an anomaly inconsistent with the original intent of the executive branch and the understanding of the Senate at the time NATO was formed. The declared purpose of sending American troops to Europe in NATO's formative period was to bolster the morale of the still weak European member states and to hold the line pending the emergence of a Western European defense capability. The subsequent expansion of Soviet military power, combined with East-West political crises— notably over Berlin—and the unresolved character of the German problem, led to a buildup and consolidation of American military and nuclear power in the European theater.

Testifying before the Senate Committee on Foreign Relations in April 1949, Secretary of State Dean Acheson was asked by Republican Senator Bourke B. Hickenlooper whether, under the pending North Atlantic Treaty, the United States would "be expected to send substantial numbers of troops over there [to Europe] as a more or less permanent contribution to the development of these countries' capacity to resist?" Acheson replied: "The answer to that question, Senator, is a clear and absolute 'No.' "[3]

In the same hearings, Secretary of Defense Louis Johnson refused to bind the administration not to send troops to Europe, although General Omar N. Bradley, Army Chief of Staff, implied that the deployment of large numbers of U.S. forces in Europe was not contemplated. He also said that he had "never made any attempt to try to figure out the number of divisions it would require to hold the Rhine River"[4] and that he had not yet gone into the question of whether "in order to hold the Rhine against a Russian crossing, it would be necessary to have American troops in addition to European troops."[5]

The Case against the Status Quo

Resistance to maintaining U.S. forces in Europe at current levels arises from multiple considerations. It would be misleading to assign these an order of importance, as they tend to converge. For purposes of discussion, they may be somewhat arbitrarily grouped according to four concerns: (1) a sense of slow but steady change in the European political environment, suggesting that the threat of armed conflict is diminishing; (2) a feeling that America's military role in Europe could be performed with substantially reduced forces; (3) impatience with the apparent unwillingness or inability of Western Europeans to assume a larger share of the defense burden; and (4) dissatisfaction with the cost of deploying American forces at current levels in Europe and with the effects of this large military presence on the balance of payments. There is a feeling that in Europe, as elsewhere, the United States is overcommitted and hence less able to manage a growing list of urgent and long-neglected domestic problems. Each of these concerns is discussed below.

The European Political Environment

President Nixon had said that the era of confrontation is yielding to one of negotiation—a judgment that a significant part of the Congress not only shares but is eager to vindicate. The point of direct American confrontation with the USSR is Europe, where the thaw in the cold war, or spirit of détente, is most apparent, where the security system seems neither expressive of nor responsive to the forces for change, and where the prospect of armed conflict between opposing and nuclear-capable forces is most remote.

During the debate on his amendment, Senator Mansfield said that

relations between all the NATO countries and the Soviet Union are excellent—first rate. Trade is good in the Eastern European countries. I think our trade amounts to $300 million and that of Western Europe amounts to $3 billion. . . . The contacts are good, economically, culturally, and socially. But it is an odd fact that every time a proposal is made in the U.S. Senate to bring about a reduction of U.S. military personnel and dependents in Western Europe, it is denounced by the Old Guard, by the oldtimers, by the people who had a vested interest in the creation of NATO.[6]

A heavy skepticism greets the worry that reductions in American forces in Europe would set off a "race to Moscow" and promote the eventual "Finlandization" of Western Europe. For some Europeans to put the issue in these terms, argue the skeptics, reflects primarily their satisfaction with the status quo and their understandable lack of incentive to advance the inevitable day when the United States begins to lighten its European military burden.

To reduce U.S. forces, they argue further, would be to recognize that a great many, though not all, of the political givens in the East-West situation are changing. In the late 1960s, a number of French Gaullists and other European critics of the status quo argued that the United States had already won the cold war, but that it still refused to draw the appropriate conclusions and insisted on maintaining the present security system in order to maximize its influence in Western Europe. Numerous Americans tend to agree.

A young lecturer at Princeton University's Woodrow Wilson School of Public and International Affairs has written:

The younger generation neither accepts the contrast with the Communist system nor understands the fear and condemnation of it. The generation of the cold war applied the word communist indiscriminately....

With only rare exceptions does anyone under thirty worry about countries "going communist." The often quoted statements by Soviet leaders dedicating the communist party to world domination are considered relics of the past. Moreover, why should we accept their definition of intentions? The fear that we might confront a monolithic international force has collapsed with the emergence of communist polycentrism, the liberalization in Eastern Europe and the Sino-Soviet conflict.[7]

In his remarks before the National Conference of Editorial Writers in October 1966, President Johnson reversed a cold war convention by estimating that German reunification would be a product of European settlement, rather than a precondition to it. Four years later, the complex German question was on the negotiating table, with discussion at numerous levels. The Brandt government and the USSR finally reached an agreement renouncing the use of force. Moreover, in return for Bonn's willingness to "respect" the Oder-Neisse as Germany's eastern frontier, the Soviet Union implicitly relinquished the right it had asserted under Articles 53 and 107 of the United Nations charter to intervene in German affairs by declaring allegiance to Article 2 of the charter, which bars external interference in the internal affairs of any state. Another German agreement renouncing the use of force has been concluded with Poland. And further movement is suggested by the four-power agreement on Berlin signed in September 1971.

Critics of U.S. force levels in Europe suggest that, even if further progress on the German question is blocked by East German rigidity and Soviet reluctance to permit a substantial alteration of the status quo, the political climate has changed. In this view, Bonn's Ostpolitik —and the discussions and contacts it elicits—tends to point up the relative political isolation of the East German regime and the somewhat greater maneuverability available to Bonn. Another example cited is the decline in cold war rhetoric—a virtual Soviet moratorium on "German revanchism." The uneven but rising interest in both Eastern and Western Europe in the old Soviet idea of a European security conference appears to reflect a reasonably broad sentiment favoring greater all-European political cooperation and, as much as possible, European solutions for European problems. Discussions underway on mutual and balanced reductions of NATO and Warsaw Pact forces may also lead to negotiations. When the recrudescence of historic Russo-Chinese disagreement is added to this, as well as Soviet preoccupation with internal difficulties, the notion of a serious Russian threat to Western Europe seems less plausible. Briefly, if there is neither entente nor convergence between Eastern and Western Europe, neither is there cold war nor the acute sense of insecurity that marked most of the first two decades after World War II.

Military Balance

The thirty-one Soviet divisions deployed in East Germany, Poland, Hungary, and Czechoslovakia may be said to serve three purposes: (1) military—to offset NATO forces; (2) police—to maintain the internal security and stability of the Soviet bloc; and (3) political—to remind Western Europe that the United States, unlike the USSR, is

not a European power and will eventually lower its European profile
and return to being primarily an American and Pacific power.

Skeptics on Capitol Hill tend to regard purposes (1) and (3) as
more properly the long-term concerns of Western Europeans. The
police function of the Soviet divisions is accepted as a perceived internal security requirement. No more than does the State Department do
many of the congressional and other critics of the status quo expect
significant reductions of the Soviet military presence in Central and
Eastern Europe. Some senators, on the other hand, believe that negotiations could lead to mutual reductions of NATO and Soviet bloc
forces. And the May 14, 1971 speech of the Soviet leader Leonid
I. Brezhnev, proposing talks on mutual reductions, clearly strengthened the stand of those who argue that a unilateral cut would narrow
the chances for the success of such a negotiation.

It would be hard to find more forcible statements of the two sides of
the issue of U.S. troops in Europe than those put forward in January
1970 by the then Under Secretary of State Elliot Richardson, who
mounted a strong and explicit case for maintaining American forces at
their current levels, and by Senator Mansfield, who replied four days
later with an equally explicit point-by-point rebuttal.

Richardson, while acknowledging that tensions in Europe have
lessened, said that the threat from the East had not receded, adding
that "only when the confrontation in Europe truly ends and a genuine
peace replaces the always precarious peace of mutual deterrence will
the role of our troops be finally accomplished."[8]

Senator Mansfield's reply took issue with the argument that the
time was not right to make a substantial reduction of U.S. forces in
Europe:

It seems to me that the time has now arrived. The Soviet Union faces serious problems in Czechoslovakia and elsewhere in Eastern Europe. If that
were not enough, there is a difficult situation to the East on the Soviet-
Chinese border. Soviet troops in Czechoslovakia, moreover, have been cut
from several hundred thousand to about 70,000. While it is regrettable that
the internal political life of that enlightened nation is again dictated by a foreign power, certain realities as they bear upon our military presence in Eu-

rope must be faced. What transpired in Czechoslovakia was not controllable in any fashion by NATO and bears no direct relationship to the question of the size of American forces assigned in Europe to that organization. . . .

The Soviet Union maintains half a million soldiers in Eastern Europe. While the Russians may ascribe this presence to a threat from the West, the fact is that the Soviet presence is also a significant factor in maintaining communist governments in power, as Czechoslovakia has so clearly illustrated. The democracies have no need of U.S. forces in order to maintain themselves within the nations of Western Europe; yet, that most significant political fact is disguised by our military presence in such great magnitude.[9]

Richardson argued, as others were to argue later in the May 1971 debate on the Mansfield amendment, that Moscow would be less likely to discuss mutual and balanced force reductions (MBFR) if it appeared that the United States would make a unilateral reduction in its forces.[10]

In reply, Senator Mansfield noted that "NATO has been studying mutual and balanced force reductions for years."[11] He pressed the point at greater length in the May 1971 debate on his amendment:

We are told that unilateral reduction of our NATO forces would doom prospects of a complementary reduction of Warsaw Pact armies. . . . That is just not so. . . . It is no secret, for instance, that Russia's need to strengthen its forces in the Far East continues more than ever today. At the same time, Russia continues to follow us in the costly and ever spiraling strategic arms race. And, no less than we, are the Soviets aware of the demands made by their entire defense budget upon the domestic economy.

For all these reasons—but primarily because of the tensions in the Far East—Moscow has a very great incentive indeed to reduce its Warsaw Pact forces and redeploy them eastward.

What makes the Russians hesitate? Clearly the dominant reason is the problem of political control in Eastern Europe. . . . If Soviet planners find their Far East concerns sufficiently pressing, some reduction in Eastern Europe no doubt would be risked. Otherwise such a reduction is unlikely under any circumstances.

So how does the size of NATO's army fit into this picture? I suggest . . . that cutting our Seventh Army forces is an equally reasonable way to induce the Soviets to reduce their manpower in the satellites. I suggest such a cut on our part would act as effectively to obtain this end as would any force reductions reached mutually through long drawn-out negotiations. It is clear, too, that with a substantial reduction of our NATO contingent, the willingness of Eastern Europe to tolerate an undiminished Soviet presence would be sharply reduced.[12]

To critics of the U.S. force posture and to many other observers, the danger of a frontal Soviet assault against Western Europe, or even of a perimeter thrust, has always seemed a low-risk possibility. A number of those who have supported the Mansfield position tend to view U.S. NATO troop commitments as more traditional than rational and as more a function of bureaucratic inertia and unwillingness to risk rocking the boat in Western Europe than an objective assessment of what is required of the United States to redress Europe's military imbalance.

When told that a primary purpose of deploying American forces in Germany is to confirm the American commitment to use nuclear weapons, if necessary, in Western Europe's defense, critics contend that one-half, or even less, the current number of uniformed hostages would serve this purpose. In answer to the argument that such reductions would lower the nuclear threshold and deprive NATO of a non-nuclear option, these critics take an essentially European view, contending that war will be avoided if the United States maintains a stable nuclear balance and deterrent.

Senator Stuart Symington of Missouri has said, "In all the years I have been connected with the military, executive branch as well as the legislative, I have never known a single military expert who felt the forces of NATO could contain a major Soviet attack against Europe without the use of nuclear weapons."[13]

The only senator who serves on both the Armed Services Committee and the Foreign Relations Committee, Symington has recommended a limit of 50,000 in the number of U.S. forces in Continental Europe. As chairman of the Foreign Relations Committee's Subcommittee on U.S. Security Agreements and Commitments Abroad, he commented thus on a committee staff tour of American military facilities in Europe and the Mediterranean: "It is significant to note that in almost every country visited they found military facilities whose original mission had long since faded."[14]

Many critics also believe that U.S. force deployments are maintained at present levels because the numbers themselves have acquired a symbolic importance in Europe that exceeds their military purpose and utility and that fortifies the tendency of national security bureaucrats to avoid rocking boats and to link existing commitments to "worst case" military contingencies.

In addition to those who favor specific force reductions in Europe, others propose a relatively undiscriminating cut in the budget for conventional or general purpose forces. An attitude of gathering strength holds that the only way to limit defense spending is to set somewhat arbitrary ceilings on the authorization requests of the three services, while extending the freedom of each to determine how best to allocate fewer resources. This tendency would almost certainly lead to greater cuts in general purpose forces than in strategic forces. If the size of conventional forces thus declined, pressures for cutting U.S. forces in Europe would surely mount still further. In this event, a progressively larger number of U.S. government officials might find the rationale for a high posture in Europe unconvincing.

Western European Burden Sharing

Impatience with the attitudes and security policies of the Western Europeans runs through the criticism voiced by many Americans in regard to their own government's position. Rightly or wrongly, they sense a European preference for an unchanging high American military posture in the area and a corresponding reluctance to take steps that would permit some rebalancing of the present NATO defense system. They believe that the Europeans can do more, and they cite supporting statements such as those by the former Assistant Secretary of Defense for Systems Analysis, Alain C. Enthoven, and his special assistant, K. Wayne Smith:

The Europeans are spending a much smaller fraction of their GNP on defense than is the United States and this fraction continues to grow smaller. In 1968, our Center Region allies spent less than 4.5 percent of their GNP on defense; the United States spent nearly 10 percent. Even excluding the Viet

Nam war (assuming that this involves an incremental cost of $20 billion per year), we still spent well over 7 percent of our GNP on defense. In terms of defense spending per capita, the United States in 1968 spent roughly six times as much as Belgium, four times as much as the Netherlands and three times as much as Great Britain and Germany, again excluding Viet Nam expenditures....

If the United States were to reduce its non-Viet Nam defense expenditures and military manpower to the average level of its NATO Center Region allies (which we do not recommend), it could reduce defense spending by over $25 billion per year and could demobilize over a million men.[15]

Critics also refer to such comparisons as those noted in a recent NATO study reporting that Soviet defense expenditures rose 5 to 6 percent a year between 1965 and 1969 but that defense spending in European NATO countries fell 4 percent in roughly the same period.[16]

Senator Symington reached a more sweeping conclusion: Since the beginning of NATO 17 years ago, no European nation has ever lived up to its military commitments. This failure on their part has always resulted in a shortage of tens of thousands of troops that had been planned for the defense of Europe.[17] And Mansfield said, in rebuttal to former Under Secretary Richardson:

It is all very well to talk about the "strength, closeness, trust, realism, and flexibility" of NATO, as Mr. Richardson did. . . . But it seems to me that there is a contrast between these words and the fact that the 250 million people of Western Europe, with tremendous industrial resources and long military experience, are unable to organize an effective military coalition to defend themselves against 200 million Russians who are contending at the same time with 800 million Chinese, but must continue after 20 years to depend on 200 million Americans for their defense. The status quo has been safe and comfortable for our European allies. But . . . it has made the Europeans less interested in their own defense. . . .

I am not arguing that there should be a larger military establishment than has been agreed to before but only that the West Germans meet their predetermined NATO commitments as we have met ours. I might say, parenthetically, that the same comment pertains to other NATO countries as well. The fact is that in terms of the percentage of armed forces to men of military age, in many NATO countries that percentage is not only below the 8.7 percent found in the United States but also below the 4 percent figure which applies to West Germany. And in all of the NATO countries that have compulsory military service—except Greece, Portugal, and Turkey—the period of service is shorter than it is in the United States.[18]

A seldom articulated attitude in some political circles is that a reduced American commitment would perforce stimulate greater European cooperation and unity, plus a correspondingly greater European commitment to joint defense. To the orthodox reply that the Western Europeans would merely emulate the Americans by doing less themselves, the skeptics suggest that if the inevitable reduction in the American military presence fails to spur the Europeans to greater effort, then it is better to discover that now rather than later. The NATO system, they suggest, cannot indefinitely sustain the anomaly of a 14–1 configuration—the 1 supporting the 14.

Senator George Aiken of Vermont, dean of Senate Republicans, reflected this sentiment during the May 1971 debate on the Mansfield amendment:

As for the Western Europeans, they have to decide how they will cope with their own defense ...

We cannot make the decision for them, nor can we any longer afford to relieve them from making a decision ...

More than enough American troops are in Europe to serve our objectives, unless, of course, our allies wish to pay for their continued presence.

A declaration by Congress on this matter, coming at a time when it seems that the British may finally be joining Europe in the Common Market, should give to that historic decision a dimension more fitting to its real importance than any net calculation of economic benefits and costs.

I assume that the Common Market aspires to be more than an association of grocers.

I assume it is a step toward Western Europe resuming responsibility for its own defense and for its own collective and distinct contribution to a better and safer world.

This is what we had hoped for when we launched the Marshall plan. This is what we had in mind when we used to talk of a United States of Europe.

The time has come to see if yesterday's hopes were justified or not.[19]

A number of senators have supported the Mansfield position, primarily on burden-sharing grounds. One of them, Republican Senator Charles H. Percy of Illinois, has said that " 'burden sharing' . . . simply means that the Europeans will begin to carry a fair share of the expenses of their own defense."[20] Senator Percy offered a list of current NATO-related American expenses that he believed could and should be passed on to Europeans. He warned: "If no satisfactory alternative [to the status quo] is implemented . . . I am prepared to help lead the fight in the Senate for troop reduction."[21]

The inevitable change in the attitudes of Americans and Europeans toward each other also influences the issue of force levels. The gradual blurring of the special character of U.S.-Western European relations increases the reluctance on Capitol Hill and elsewhere to continue bearing what seems to be a disproportionate share of the defense burden and appearing to assign greater importance to European security than do the Europeans themselves. Europe's recovery from the war, followed by various experiments in unity—notably the formation and development of the European Economic Community (Common Market)—gripped America's imagination, especially in the early 1960s, when a plethora of books on European integration issued from the academic community and Jean Monnet was accorded the cover of *Time*. However, the Common Market is seen in 1971 less as a precursor to a united Europe capable one day of joining with North America to make the world safer and better than as a trading bloc whose members agree on little more than restrictive agricultural policies and uncongenial preference arrangements with third countries. Early in 1970, J. Robert Schaetzel, U.S. Representative to the European Community, commented that "the immediate response to the question 'what does America think today of the European Community?' must be, 'it does not think about it very much.' "[22]

This changing American attitude toward Europe sharpens U.S. impatience with Europe's apparent indifference to security matters and thus with America's NATO troop commitments. And matters are not helped by Western Europe's greater freedom and incentive to trade with Eastern Europe. As Senator Symington has observed, "We are the only country that does not make a major effort to improve trade behind the Iron Curtain. I do not understand why the United States continues to pick up the tab for a large portion of NATO defense, at the same time the countries we are defending build up trade relations with Iron Curtain countries and we do not."[23]

Symington emphasized East-West trade; others who share his view on the burden-sharing issue are bothered by different problems on the NATO agenda. The resurgence of protectionist sentiment in Washington, for example, is in large measure a reaction to the policies of the Common Market. Such sentiment in turn influences congressional opinion on defending Europe, as well as the calculations of the executive branch as it seeks to reconcile perceived requirements of European security with the dynamics of its relations with Congress, the fate of various legislative programs, and so forth.

The mutually hostile attitudes of Americans and Western Europeans to aspects of each other's trade policies are reinforced by emerging political divergences. In the Middle East, for example, what has appeared to be American backing of Israel in a proxy confrontation with the Soviet Union has aroused little sympathy from European NATO governments, some of which chafe at their inability to exercise greater influence in a part of the world that is historically central to their interests. In turn, Europe's unwillingness to bolster or effectively complement American efforts, or to treat Middle East issues on American terms, is another point of difference, though it is relatively subtle and seldom articulated.

Divergence in U.S. and European interests is neither new nor surprising. The impact of such divergence on defense relations is not yet calculable, but if, in order to save money and avoid unnecessary risks, it appears clearly desirable to reduce American overseas defense spending, the distinction between commitments in Europe and those in other parts of the world is likely to fade, at least outside the executive branch. Elsewhere, the chief concern is budgetary and the highest priorities, domestic.

Cost

If any single argument against the American military posture in Europe unites the critics, it is the issue of cost. President Nixon's decision on August 15, 1971 to suspend the dollar's convertibility into gold and to impose an import surcharge will change the framework within which this issue will be debated, but it will not put the issue to rest. On the contrary, administration spokesmen have specifically included American defense costs abroad as an element to be considered in the negotiation of new international monetary arrangements. And Senator Mansfield, in commenting on the President's measures to protect the dollar, said that the U.S. economy "could be further helped by cutting down the U.S. defense commitment in Europe."

The financial issue involves both the foreign exchange and budgeting costs, as is evident from the following statement by Senator Mansfield, who joins Senators Symington and Percy in strenuously questioning the direct costs of force deployments in Europe, as well as the consequent charge on the balance of payments:

There are 310,000 American troops in Europe, some 230,000 dependents and about 14,000 civilian employees. Thus, there are, in total, over 550,000 Americans in Europe today either serving in the military or connected with the military. In 1969, our direct outlays in Europe reached a new high of over $1.6 billion and, in Germany alone, a new high of almost $950 million. ... These expenditures ... represent a drain on the dollar and act to weaken its international position. Salaries and other indirect costs eat heavily into U.S. tax resources, leaving less for essential purposes at home and adding severe inflationary pressures to the economy.[24]

These are convincing numbers to Americans who are already sympathetic to the argument that it would make sense to bring home and demobilize some portion of the European-based forces.

In the early and middle 1960s, the balance-of-payments effects of the Seventh Army and other European-based American forces were offset chiefly by West German procurement of American military equipment. From fiscal year 1968 on, the offset agreements provided for a mixture of military procurement and German purchases of U.S.

securities, and included a West German pledge that dollar reserves would not be converted into gold.

Senators Mansfield and Symington did not seem reassured by these revised offset arrangements. Mansfield concedes that they have produced some improvement in the balance of payments, but he also observes that

while the amount of foreign exchange inflow involved is higher, so is the foreign exchange gap because it becomes more expensive every year to keep our forces in Germany. With the revaluation of the German mark, moreover, this expense stated in dollars will increase again, and, possibly, more drastically than in the past.[25]

And Senator Symington observed, during the debate on the Mansfield amendment:

U.S. defense expenditures in Western Europe which entered the international balance of payments in the fiscal year 1970 totaled $1.731 billion, the highest figure ever for such expenditures.

In order to place this figure in perspective, let us note that our balance-of-payments deficit in 1970 on a liquidity basis was $3.85 billion; therefore, our military expenditures in Western Europe accounted for 46.1 percent of all that deficit. If military sales to Western Europe, which I am informed totaled $599 million in 1970, are deducted from the $1.77 billion of military expenditures in Western Europe, net military expenditures still constitute 30.5 percent of the total balance-of-payments deficit in 1970.[26]

The concern with offset has shifted since 1969 to the old issue of budgetary support and qualitative improvements in European NATO forces. A "defense improvement program," to which ten European NATO governments committed themselves in late 1970, channels an additional $1 billion over a five-year period into NATO infrastructure. This action will not reduce NATO-related costs to the United States; it represents, rather, a modest increase in European defense efforts. For this and other reasons, congressional critics are not impressed by this joint European declaration. They plainly feel that the ten European defense ministers, after long and arduous consultation, brought forth a mouse. The concern about costs is sharpened by allegations of "fat" in the Seventh Army, but the responsible military

officials argue that the German-based conventional U.S. forces have
been pared to the bone.

Related Concerns

Increasingly, the dispute over costs, burden sharing, the military balance, and the Soviet threat reflects concerns only tangentially related
to the level of U.S. forces in Europe. One of these has already been
cited: the divergence between U.S. and European views on political
and economic questions. Two others deserve special note: the nature
and utility of American tactical nuclear weapons deployed in the European theater, and the reordering of American priorities and adapt-
ing America's world role.

Tactical Nuclear Weapons

Unease about tactical nuclear weapons affects the troop issue.
Some members of Congress who believe that the executive branch has
maintained these weapons at a level far in excess of any conceivable
need conclude, by analogy, that the level of U.S. conventional forces
is also unnecessarily high. In both cases, they think that inertia in the
executive branch discourages efforts to lower commitments by matching them more closely with actual requirements.

Little information is available to the public or to the Congress
about nuclear forces in the European theater that are assigned to
NATO and controlled by the United States. The number of tactical
nuclear weapons deployed on land and sea in the European theater has
been reliably estimated at more than 7,000 and the number of delivery
systems at about 2,250. These include tactical aircraft, ballistic missiles (Pershing and Sergeant), short-range missiles, and artillery
tubes. The exact military significance of the number and character of
these weapons is obscured by tight security regulations. Members of
the Senate Foreign Relations Committee, for example, complain of
being denied information obviously available to the Soviet Union

about nuclear weapons in the European theater. Executive branch witnesses are not only reluctant to discuss such weapons but on occasion have disclosed that they had instructions not to discuss them at all.[27]

More important than executive secrecy are the substantive concerns that disturb congressmen. Some claim that a great many of these European-based tactical nuclear systems are highly vulnerable to preemptive attack and are hence unstable, and that a number of allegedly dual-capable weapons systems in Europe—especially the forward-based aircraft—are available only in their nuclear mode. Some also question the putative requirement for large deployments of the weapons; they regard the tactical nuclear option as more theoretical, or even fanciful, than real, and refer to such experts as Enthoven and Smith, who write that the idea of a limited nuclear war

ignores a basic lesson that the leaders of the U.S. Government in all cold-war crises have learned—that when faced with the decision to start a nuclear war, almost any other alternative looks better; and it is too risky to serve as the foundation for a preferred strategy. . . .

. . . from a European standpoint, there is likely to be little difference between a so-called "tactical" nuclear war and a strategic war. . . . In addition, there would be great pressure to escalate the war by attacking fixed targets such as airfields, logistic installations, lines of communications and rear areas where enemy nuclear delivery systems would be located.[28]

And Carl Kaysen, Director of the Institute for Advanced Studies, Princeton University, and a former deputy special assistant for national security affairs under President Kennedy, argues that "units now manning a large variety of tactical nuclear weapons could usefully be viewed as even more redundant than the ground combat forces."[29]

Such statements reflect a widely held opinion that if fighting between NATO and Warsaw Pact forces could not be confined to or resolved at the nonnuclear level, it would either bypass or swiftly escalate beyond the tactical nuclear stage into a strategic nuclear war between the United States and the Soviet Union. This view feeds existing unease over the European-based nuclear weapons and strengthens, for reasons that are more a matter of instinct than logic, the argument for reducing conventional forces.

Priorities

The growing concern over priorities, while not strictly germane to the issue of U.S. troops in Europe, influences the views of those seeking to reduce this commitment. American attitudes toward the U.S. role in the world are clearly under review. Both the character and scope of U.S. overseas activities are being questioned. Numerous critics argue that things other than numbers of divisions, most of all the conduct of domestic affairs, affect Europe's judgment of American leadership. Thus, they suggest that issues of European security should be seen in the wider perspective of social questions and the national goals that must be pursued if ultimately America is to preserve its social and political system. Such thinking has often been voiced by Senator J. W. Fulbright, chairman of the Foreign Relations Committee. He has said, for example:

Every nation has a double identity: it is both a *power* engaged in foreign relations and a *society* serving the interests of its citizens. As a *power* the nation draws upon but does not replenish its people's economic, political and moral resources. The replenishment of wealth—in this broader than economic sense—is a function of domestic life, of the nation as a society. In the last three decades the United States has been heavily preoccupied with its role as the world's greatest power, to the neglect of its societal responsibilities, and at incalculable cost to our national security. The economic cost is reflected in the disparity of almost ten to one between federal military expenditures since World War II and regular national budgetary expenditures for education, welfare, health and housing. The political cost is reflected in the steady concentration of power in the hands of the national executive, in a long-term trend toward authoritarian government. The moral cost is reflected in the unhappiness of the American people, most particularly in the angry alienation of our youth.[30]

And in a committee hearing in June 1970, Senator Fulbright said: "It really seems to me the stability of the United States at the moment—or its instability—is a much greater hazard to the future of Europe than a Russian invasion."[31]

The question of priorities cuts deep. It was once axiomatic that the Congress would not assign priorities to requests for funds by reducing one program in order to strengthen another, but this may no longer be the case. Congressional attitudes are changing, especially in the Senate. Whether the change will be permanent, whether it will ever create a predictable majority on a given combination of defense-related issues, is far from clear. What does seem clear is that the executive branch must now reckon with a qualitative change in the congressional mood and must anticipate considerably closer scrutiny of military spending in general, and of all overseas commitments in particular.

As for the issue of our European deployment, Senator Mansfield's warning, issued just before the vote that defeated his amendment, seems certain to be vindicated in one way or another:

Sometimes it takes a sledge hammer to make an imprint and place an issue on the table. I did raise this issue. I have been raising it for 11 years. . . . The issue has been made, and regardless of the outcome of the vote tonight, it will not disappear. It will not return to the cobwebs where it has rested so peacefully for the past two decades and 1 year.[32]

2

Soviet Policy

DESPITE traditional Soviet hostility to America's military presence and political weight in Europe, the prospect of a reduction of U.S. troops on the Continent arouses little overt reaction from Moscow. Many Americans who advocate cutting these forces assume that the question has no important bearing on Soviet policy. They argue that the move need not adversely affect the European political balance and might even induce the Soviet Union to scale down its own military presence in Eastern Europe.[1] Indeed, some critics of orthodox thinking on force level issues go much further; they assert that whatever the goals of Soviet policy elsewhere, in Europe the Russians seek little more than Western acceptance of the political status quo and in fact have shown a genuine desire to move, if gradually, away from harsh cold war confrontation toward greater cooperation between the two halves of Europe.[2]

Such assumptions can neither be proved nor disproved by Moscow's recent endorsement of negotiations on mutual and balanced force reductions (MBFR). Nor has the normally guarded Soviet attitude on the issue of U.S. troop levels in Europe shed much light. It may reflect division and uncertainty within the Kremlin; it may also suggest a judicious reluctance to risk the consequences of interfering in the

American domestic political debate. Equally, the MBFR initiative may mean either that the Soviet Union now wants to bring about mutual reductions, or that talks about force levels are now regarded by Secretary Brezhnev and his colleagues as a diplomatic device of some utility so long as the talks do not lead very far. The point is that we don't know. Moscow seems to be embarked on a well-orchestrated, multifaceted peace offensive focused particularly, though not exclusively, on Europe. But little can be gained by trying to establish the precise aims of Soviet diplomacy at any given moment, as these are seldom clear.[3]

Nonetheless, the possibility of a U.S. troop reduction demands a close examination of the trends in recent Soviet policy toward Europe. This chapter considers overall Soviet policy toward Europe, the possible effects of U.S. troop reductions on that policy, and the likely Soviet course if present U.S. force levels are maintained.

Soviet Policy toward Europe

Détente, of course, has been a basic ingredient of Soviet foreign policy rhetoric from Lenin's time to the present day. The Russians have repeatedly proclaimed periods of peaceful coexistence with the West; but none of these interludes has produced a negotiated settlement of major political differences.

Nevertheless, it can be argued that the present Soviet leaders have compelling reasons for promoting détente. According to this view, the men in the Kremlin are cautious pragmatists, innocent of ideological zeal. As calculating realists, the argument continues, they are sensitive to Russia's economic weakness, and seek both Western economic and technical assistance and some means of setting limits on spending for strategic armament. Moreover, they must contend for the foreseeable future with Chinese pressure on their inner-Asian borders, another factor arguing for a genuine relaxation of tensions with the West.

Compared with Nikita Khrushchev, today's Soviet leaders do appear to be ideologically less militant, considerably grayer in style, and altogether more circumspect in behavior. Far more than Stalin, Khrushchev was prepared to commit Soviet power and prestige to dangerous ventures in the ideologically rooted conviction that bold strokes and timely risks would hasten the triumph of communism on "the global scale." But the scope of Khrushchev's enterprises exceeded Soviet resources, whether political or military. And toward the end of his rule and in studied defiance of the Chinese, the flamboyant Soviet leader seems to have inclined toward acceptance of the East-West balance that he himself had so strenuously tried to overturn. By contrast, his successors have been not only less erratic but also more persistent and activist than Khrushchev in his final period. Moreover, they have succeeded where Khrushchev failed (or rather was not granted time to succeed)—that is, in forging a strategic and conventional military capacity that equips the Soviet Union with the attributes of a global military power.

Although the present Soviet leaders appear to lack Khrushchev's ideological élan, they must be acknowledged to have developed the functional equivalent in the form of a great-power consciousness, deeply colored by Russian chauvinism. The latter characteristic serves them well at home, by lending a sense of urgency to their insistence on social and political discipline and by imparting a semblance of great purpose to their otherwise lackluster bureaucratic rule. As undistinguished and sometimes timorous products of an impersonal machine, always sensitive to competing domestic bureaucratic pressures, the Soviet leaders have a vested interest in forward movement on the international scene that ought never to be underestimated.

At the same time, whatever advantages the Brezhnev/Kosygin government may expect from a policy of peaceful coexistence with the West, its conception of détente is conditional. An atmosphere of unlimited détente could erode Soviet hegemony in Eastern Europe. Moreover, given Soviet neo-authoritarianism at home, the Kremlin is more sensitive than ever to the potentially subversive ramifications within the Soviet Union itself of a full-scale relaxation of international tensions. Small wonder that, much like Khrushchev in his day, the present Soviet leaders continue to inveigh against "ideological co-existence" and have sought even more self-consciously than Khrushchev—especially since the Czechoslovak experience—to orchestrate détente so as to arrest its potentially disruptive effects in Eastern Europe.

This is not to minimize Soviet perceptions of important areas of potential agreement between the Soviet Union and the United States, notably their common interest in avoiding nuclear war and in controlling the cost of the arms race. It is, rather, to stress the persistence not only of a Soviet desire to achieve this agreement, but also of a more complex Soviet conception of détente than is perceived by many in the West—a conception that may vary among elite groups in the Soviet Union. In addition, attention should be called to the likelihood of different levels and differentiated degrees of détente—between the Soviet Union and the United States, on the one hand, where limited accommodations based on congruent interests need not exclude political competition and conflict, and between the Soviet Union and Western Europe, on the other, where cooperative ventures need not rule out efforts to expand Soviet political influence.

In contrast to Khrushchev's grandiose and largely undifferentiated global perspective, the Soviet leaders today are again concentrating on Europe as the "central front" of Soviet involvement in world politics.[4] Soviet commentators treat Europe's division between East and West as inherently unstable and potentially explosive.[5] They make no secret of the Kremlin's view of the European theater as an arena of both threat and opportunity: threat in the latent political challenge to Soviet hegemony over Eastern Europe, opportunity in the prospect of spreading Soviet influence into the West.[6] While this is not a new perception, it has renewed relevance arising from Moscow's apparent belief in the emergence of exceptionally favorable circumstances. These are said to be the result of "the historical changes in Europe in favor of the peace forces and the failure of the plans harbored by the Atlantic strategists to perpetuate the cold war and the 'positions of strength' policy."[7] To put matters more bluntly, as Moscow sees it,

Western drift and disorientation may be used to gain fresh political advantages in Western Europe, while consolidating the Soviet Union's control over its own allies in Eastern Europe.

The persistent if cautious pursuit of these two (always potentially contradictory) objectives is the thrust of current Soviet policy toward Europe[8]—for example, in urging that a European security conference be held in the hope of gaining formal Western recognition of the status quo and in seeking to use this and related initiatives to weaken Western unity, while simultaneously trying to strengthen the Warsaw Pact. On the one hand, Moscow calls for improved East-West economic relations; on the other, it uses this appeal both to try to discourage closer Western European integration and to pressure the Eastern Europeans to greater cooperative efforts within the Council for Economic Mutual Assistance, bluntly warning them not to exceed certain bounds in their trade relations with the West. Similarly, the Kremlin endorses scientific and cultural cooperation with the West, while striving to limit intellectual contacts. The aim is to acquire Western technological know-how without risking infection with Western social and political ideas.

Consider the importance that Moscow currently attaches to the proposed conference on European security and cooperation. At first glance, this project may seem a curious retread of Soviet cold war diplomacy of the fifties, when Moscow's objectives were to block the rearmament of West Germany and discourage the establishment of the European Defense Community. By 1965–66, when the Kremlin revived its European security scheme, the political environment had changed in a number of ways. Notwithstanding divisive trends in the communist world, Soviet strategic power was on the verge of a major expansion; the West appeared to be in serious political trouble, owing to de Gaulle's independent foreign policy, West Germany's continued political weaknesses (if not disarray), and America's involvement in Vietnam. If Moscow had been genuinely worried about a Western threat to Soviet security in the mid-fifties, it had far less cause for concern a decade later.

It is not far-fetched to regard the Soviet Union's revival of the European security project as an attempt to wrest the diplomatic initiative from a badly divided West. Probably Moscow's hope was not to gain acceptance of its specific proposals, but rather to achieve broad political advantage through a psychologically timely appeal—and to do this without sacrificing its position in Eastern Europe. This observation is strengthened by recalling what happened to the European security project once Moscow decided, in early 1967, that the readiness of West Germany's "grand coalition" government to associate itself with the quest for détente in Europe might pose a serious challenge to Soviet policy in Eastern Europe. In effect, the Soviet proposal for a European security conference was transformed into a narrow appeal against alleged "West German militarism, revanchism, and neo-Nazism." If nothing else, that remarkable Soviet turnabout confirms the absolute priority that Moscow has always accorded the preservation of its own power sphere in Eastern Europe.[9]

In this sense, the invasion of Czechoslovakia and that country's gradual "normalization" to Moscow's satisfaction were a precondition to reviving the Soviet diplomatic offensive. One cannot know for certain what considerations prompted the Soviet Union and its allies to call again in March 1969 for a European security conference; but it can be safely assumed that troubles with China played a relatively minor role, and that even Moscow's understandable wish to efface the stigma of Czechoslovakia and perhaps gain indirect Western sanction for that move is not the full story. What may be said is that in 1966 or today, the least of Moscow's concerns in pressing new European security proposals is anxiety about Soviet security. "On the whole, our positions in Europe are secure," Foreign Minister Gromyko observed in 1969,[10] and his confidence has been echoed repeatedly since then. As one ranking Soviet commentator put it, "Unlike the thirties, today it is a matter not of military and political measures to eliminate the threat of aggression, but of *political steps to exclude the very emergence of such a threat*."[11] In other words, the goal is nothing less than a new set of political relationships in Europe.

In the Soviet view, any new set of political relationships must be based on Western recognition of the status quo in Eastern Europe, in-

cluding recognition of East Germany. "The division of Europe on social and political lines, that is, the division into states belonging to
opposite systems, is a natural result of the European nations' advance
along the road of social progress and in this sense it is historically irreversible."[12] Small wonder that Western suggestions that the proposed European security conference might profitably discuss relations
among the socialist states are denounced in Moscow.[13] Soviet spokesmen may propose the eventual dissolution of both NATO and the
Warsaw Pact organization in some novel Continent-wide security
system, but important elements in the Soviet leadership also insist
that "it would be absurd to expect the socialist states to prepare right
away for a gradual 'dismantling' of the Warsaw Treaty. On the contrary, they are forced to show concern for strengthening and improving their militant alliance."[14]

Nor is this idle rhetoric. The presence of Soviet troops in East Germany, Poland, Czechoslovakia, and Hungary, whether under Warsaw
Pact commitments or bilateral arrangements, still constitutes the ultimate guarantee of the integrity of the "socialist camp" in Europe,
especially in its crucial northern tier (East Germany, Poland, Czechoslovakia, and Hungary). The same Russian troops also serve notice
on Western Europe that the Soviet Union, unlike the United States,
should be regarded as a permanently involved European military
power. Finally, there is abundant evidence that Moscow views the
Warsaw Pact as a vehicle for political coordination among the alliance
partners. Some signs in recent years—the reform of the Pact's command structure in 1969, the Pact's joint "brotherhood in arms" military exercises in the autumn of 1970—suggest that the Kremlin is
using the alliance framework to limit the political maneuverability of
the Pact's outstanding dissident, Romania.[15]

Thus, when Soviet spokesmen refer to "eliminating the division of
Europe into military political groupings," they still mean primarily the
dissolution of NATO. Hence, Moscow reacted negatively to Western counterproposals on European security that involve what it calls
the "bloc to bloc approach." Similarly, the USSR was wary of linking mutual force reductions to the proposed European security con-

ference, ostensibly because the issue should not be torn out of the "fabric of other great issues of disarmament."

The Soviet Union began moving from this position in June 1970, when it conceded that the question of "reducing foreign armed forces on the territory of European states" might be discussed in "an all-European security commission to be set up by the conference or in any other forum acceptable to the interested states."[16] This may have been primarily a tactic aimed at preventing the West from using its demand for mutual and balanced force reductions (MBFR) to block a European security conference.

By the spring of 1971, however, Moscow was viewing MBFR in broader terms—possibly as a major element in a venturesome diplomacy that would link reciprocal force reductions with such other issues as the strategic arms limitation talks (SALT), Berlin, talks among the five nuclear powers and, tacitly perhaps, with the broader question of Europe's political orientation. At the Twenty-fourth Soviet Party Congress in March 1971, Secretary Brezhnev proposed a reduction of armed forces in Central Europe. Soon afterward, he and other Soviet leaders began calling more specifically for negotiations aimed at MBFR. Especially notable was his statement on this subject in mid-1971, just as the Mansfield amendment was coming to a vote in the Congress. Nor was the ideological flank of the peace offensive neglected. For example, Moscow's leading Americanologist, Georgi A. Arbatov, justified the quest for better relations with the United States by citing Lenin to the effect that communists should distinguish between those in the West "who lean toward a military solution of problems" and those who "lean toward pacifism, even of the most insignificant kind."[17]

Although these Soviet proposals, including the MBFR initiative, are advanced in broad and unspecific terms, the response from Washington and other Western capitals has been positive—and that is as it should be. A widening process of negotiation on sensitive political and defense issues could promote stability and strengthen the base for further progress. The 1971 Berlin agreement is a step in this direction.

An underlying purpose of Soviet policy remains, however, to discourage challenges to Soviet control in Eastern Europe and to expand Soviet influence in Western Europe.[18] Moscow's interests would benefit if increased Soviet contacts with individual Western European states regarding the European security project, or with the United States regarding MBFR, were to divide the West. This suggests that Western contacts with Moscow on potentially negotiable issues should proceed both from a perception of where interests coincide and from a recognition that the two sides' motives for negotiating may differ widely.

Soviet endorsement of expanded economic, scientific, and cultural ties with the West should be seen in the same light. It is clear that compelling economic pressures push Moscow to expand trade with the West and to enlarge its access to Western development capital and technology; that Russia's Eastern European clients are even more strongly drawn toward Western Europe's goods and know-how; and that Soviet endorsement of broadened East-West economic ties serves to sanction limited access to Western goods and capital. Yet, to cite a recent expression of a deep-rooted Soviet view, "The foreign economic policy of the socialist states does not take shape only in response to production and economic needs; primary consideration is given to the possible social and political consequences of any given contacts with capitalist countries."[19] Thus, in addressing Eastern Europe, Moscow emphasizes the limits on developing economic relations with the West and explicitly cautions that "in any development of economic cooperation with capitalist countries, the socialist countries cannot permit relaxation of control over their own economy, limitation of their freedom of action in relations with their capitalist partners, or any threat to the security of individual socialist states or the socialist community as a whole."[20] On this as on many other issues, Moscow judges what is permissible in the interests of "the socialist community as a whole" and would prefer to have East-West trade channeled through the Soviet Union.

Addressing Western Europe, Moscow identifies the United States as the "number one enemy" of East-West economic, scientific, and technical ties, and emphasizes American fears of a "weakening of

NATO and Western Europe's ties with the United States."[21] Moscow proposes that Western Europe recover its "traditional markets and raw material sources" in the East as an alternative both to the restrictiveness of the EEC and to "dangerous one-sided dependence on the United States."[22] Moscow also suggests that various East-West economic links, such as Soviet gas and oil deliveries to Western Europe, will pave the way for closer political ties between the Soviet Union and Western buyers.[23] Furthermore, while conceding the desirability of multilateral Western European economic and technical participation in certain major industrial projects—for example, automobile production in the Soviet Union—the Kremlin also appeals to individual Western European countries in an effort to stimulate a race among them for Soviet and Eastern European markets. Lest such appeals appear totally materialistic, Moscow has sought to leaven them by selectively flattering the cultural endowments of individual Western European nations. Thus, one hears expressions of appreciation for the glories of Italy, of respect for the grandeur of France, of admiration for the cultural achievements of the German nation—all directed toward refurbishing Russia's image as a European nation and, indeed, as the protagonist of European civilization against anti-European cultural "fatalism" fostered by adherents of Atlanticism, led by the United States.[24]

This line indicates a continuation of the long-term Soviet policy of dividing the West, but on closer inspection it also shows a significant shift of geopolitical emphasis. Whereas a few years ago Soviet analysts anticipated an erosion of Western positions on the fringes of Europe,[25] their attention has now moved from the periphery to the very center of the Continent. At least for the moment, Moscow apparently has concluded that the situation of "NATO flanks from the Greek black colonels' regime in the south to Norway and Denmark in the north"[26] makes the immediate political outlook on those flanks rather unfavorable. The Scandinavian countries are currently of concern because of their interest in closer ties with the Common Market. (In addition to Norway and Denmark, neutral Sweden repeatedly has been cautioned about such ties in a manner resembling the warnings

issued to Austria, but in a tone suggesting that Scandinavia is politically far more worrisome to Moscow.) At another edge of the Continent, Spain, by renewing its base agreement with the United States,
is viewed as having moved completely under NATO dominance.[27]

As for Britain, the Conservative government's foreign policy, especially its quest for admission to the Common Market, has drawn this
comment from Moscow: "To count on Britain, which is now knock-
ing on the door of the Western European 'community,' to raise the
flag of rebellion against the United States" would be "naïve."[28] Italy
seems more promising. While criticizing Italian foreign policy as
"not always consistent," Soviet commentators have noted domestic social turmoil, weak national government, and residual political strength
on the left as factors making for "greater realism" in Italian foreign
policy, which might lead to "better relations and broader cooperation
with the socialist world."[29] But even more than on Italy, present Soviet policy concentrates on the two countries at the heart of the
Continent: Germany and France.

Soviet policy toward Germany has undergone a major reversal with
far-ranging implications. From the mid-fifties until very recently,
Moscow's efforts were aimed at isolating West Germany by excluding it from European détente. The tenacity of this campaign discouraged speculation that it might be a tactic of intimidation, subject to
change whenever conditions appeared propitious to Moscow.[30] Yet
the Soviet-West German treaty of August 1970 marked just such a
shift, and the change of Soviet attitude that preceded it can be largely
explained by Chancellor Brandt's Eastern policy (Ostpolitik). After
the invasion of Czechoslovakia, which was a setback to the Federal
Republic's quest for rapprochement with Eastern Europe, Bonn decided that it had no choice but to maneuver toward détente by chan-
neling its approaches to Eastern Europe more directly through Moscow and by scaling down German objectives.

However sensible it was, Bonn's decision conferred some tactical
advantages on Moscow. Concessions on Germany's eastern frontiers
and acceptance of the principle of two German states may have been
overdue, but they are also irreversible. Soviet undertakings to Bonn,

on the other hand, whether they concern Berlin or improving intra-German contacts, can be withdrawn at any time. This clearly is how Soviet spokesmen view the matter; they suggest repeatedly that the burden of proof of further honorable intentions rests squarely with the Federal Republic.[31] In other words, the present state of Soviet-German relations gives Moscow the choice of pursuing bilateral arrangements with Bonn or of reverting to its efforts to isolate the Federal Republic. Of course it is conceivable that Moscow will alternately try both.

Ostpolitik may eventually return important dividends to the West. They might include détente with Eastern Europe, stability in Berlin, and, more particularly, the rapprochement with East Germany that Bonn is seeking. But for this to happen would mean that Ostpolitik had produced effects well beyond those favored by the present Soviet leaders. That this is clearly the object of the policy only underlines the point that the USSR and the West approach these negotiations with differing objectives—a fact that is neither unusual nor a deterrent to their successful conclusion.

The Soviet Union may also use its new relationship with Germany to seek greater leverage with France. Such efforts are already apparent. In the wake of the Soviet-German treaty, France is appealed to as a great power and a "natural pillar" of European security in the West, balancing the Soviet Union in the East. This goes hand in hand with exhortations to French business interests not to be left behind in the race to open up Soviet markets;[32] Franco-German political and economic rivalry for Soviet favor is attractive to Moscow in its own right and is seen as one of the most promising wedges against Western unity.

The foregoing analysis presents what may seem a gloomy outlook. Yet while caution may be the better part of wisdom in assessing Moscow's intentions, it is also true that pressures within the Soviet system may gradually lead to a genuine interest in accommodation with the West. Although détente-oriented rhetoric and proposals for a European security conference and talks on MBFR may be primarily tactical, some elements within the Soviet system may wish to seek a settlement with the West on mutually acceptable terms. Indeed, the tactics of détente and conference diplomacy may represent the common ground between traditional hard liners and more moderate elements in Moscow. And the latter's influence may be increased if the major Western capitals, in reacting to Moscow's initiatives, decide to explore and probe for elements of reasonableness beneath the standard wrappings, and thus deal with Soviet proposals on their individual merits, instead of treating the East's proposals as aspects of a single intractable purpose and thus rejecting them out of hand.

Effects of U.S. Force Reductions

What role in European affairs is the Soviet Union willing to concede to the United States? Although the "crisis of Atlanticism" (interpreted as the clash between American efforts to preserve political hegemony over Western Europe and the separate national interests of the individual Western European states)[33] is part of the Moscow litany, both the NATO alliance and America's political role on the Continent are treated with respect. Soviet public pronouncements, whether concerning the vitality or weaknesses of the Atlantic alliance, tend to be sober and realistic. Indeed, Soviet commentators have closely followed recent efforts to improve coordination within NATO and have recorded with some dismay signs of a recurrence of "Atlantic fever" —their term for American actions aimed at countering Soviet diplomatic initiatives in Europe.[34] Besides recognizing America's military presence and political weight, Moscow also acknowledges U.S. financial and corporate involvement in Europe. As one Soviet writer put it, "Some $20 billion of U.S. capital investment in Western Europe, like the Pentagon's 7,500 nuclear warheads under NATO auspices—this U.S. 'contribution' provides adequate testimony that it will be extremely difficult for the Western half of our continent to free itself from the protective hand of its overseas patron."[35]

This does not mean, of course, that Moscow is resigned to perpetual American political influence in Europe or indifferent to changes in the way it is exercised. Soviet policy alternates between pursuing selective détente with the United States, excluding Western Europe, and seeking cooperation with Western Europe at the expense of the United States. Soviet diplomacy manipulates the two approaches rather adroitly, always with a view to undermining the American-European relationship. The Soviet appeals for a European security conference are a case in point; they are accompanied by broad hints that developments in Soviet-American relations might make existing security arrangements and the NATO structure obsolete. At the same time, the Soviet Union and its allies have been ambiguous about U.S. participation in a European security conference. Their stated willingness to include the United States (and Canada) need not imply Soviet acceptance of a permanent U.S. role in the novel security arrangements that Moscow seeks to advance for the Continent. Similarly, Soviet diplomacy has been deliberately vague about the precise features of those arrangements, leaving it to the West, but particularly to the United States, to formulate terms and to set preconditions —which Soviet propaganda in turn seeks to exploit as evidence that Washington is determined to impose obstacles to détente in Europe.

Even more revealing is Moscow's reaction to the shift in the U.S. role in Europe envisaged by the Nixon administration's emphasis on partnership and a "low profile." The application of this policy to Europe (or "the Europeanization of the cold war," in current Soviet parlance) has set off expressions of alarm in Moscow. Soviet commentators have repeatedly denounced this approach as a gimmick to make America's allies foot the bill for preserving American hegemony in Western Europe and a device for perpetuating partition of the Continent. Typically they conclude that these efforts are doomed to failure.

More genuine distress seems to arise from an assessment of what might ensue should Washington's formula of partnership, strength, and negotiation actually work. In the traditionally conservative Soviet view, undiminished Western strength, refashioned on a more equitable division of labor, would substantially reduce the advantages flowing to Moscow from bilateral or multilateral negotiations with the West and all but eliminate any prospect of a major Soviet diplomatic breakthrough. As always, Moscow fears greater Western European political cooperation, possibly leading to more effective regional integration, for the attraction it might exert on Eastern Europe. Small wonder that a Soviet commentator has spoken apprehensively of a "Pan-Europe" without Russia.[36] Short of that political disaster, the prospects of improved Western military cooperation and some redistribution of NATO's defense burden arouse thoughts of a quasi-autonomous European political-military grouping that might be more resistant than ever to divisive Soviet pressures. Indeed, Moscow may well conceive of a German political-military role in an integrated Western Europe that would limit the returns on further overtures toward détente with Bonn, while leaving the Federal Republic relatively invulnerable to a resumption of Soviet political warfare.

For all these reasons (but perhaps especially because of the German problem), the Kremlin may be of several minds about a unilateral reduction of U.S. conventional forces on the Continent. As noted, the issue has aroused little direct Soviet comment. This suggests a measure of ambivalence in Moscow. What comment there has been makes the familiar and predictable points that American forces in Europe ought to be reduced, if not entirely withdrawn, because their presence is anachronistic, unnecessary, and dangerous—anachronistic because "it is 1970 and not 1949";[37] unnecessary because "the new tendency of European politics that finds expression particularly in the signing of the USSR-Federal Republic of Germany treaty removes all justification for the presence of almost a third of a million American soldiers in Europe";[38] and dangerous because the very presence of so large an American contingent threatens to implicate Western Europe in American commitments and conflicts outside Europe.[39]

So much for the conventional themes. More thoughtful Soviet analysis, of which even less has been made public, may run along somewhat different though still ambivalent lines; indeed, Soviet leaders may hold differing views on this point. On the negative side, to the degree that Moscow relies on the presence of U.S. troops as an exploitable irritant, their reduction would diminish a valuable source of propaganda; and there is always a question whether Moscow would welcome the relatively larger German role in NATO that would follow U.S. withdrawals. But these considerations cannot be compared with the presumed advantages to Moscow of a precipitous unilateral American withdrawal, a step that might undermine Western European confidence in U.S. commitments and create large openings for Soviet pressure. It is probably with that prospect in mind that Soviet commentators have invitingly suggested that American troop withdrawals might reduce the risk of nuclear war in Europe.[40]

Seen from Moscow, the prospect of a closely knit Atlantic grouping, with Western Europe tightly linked to the United States, has almost vanished. Although U.S.-oriented Atlanticism is still defined as inimical to Soviet interests, Moscow now purports to fear that a redistribution of the Western defense burden could strengthen the integrative process in a Western Europe still linked to the United States along many crucial lines. This underlies the hostile Soviet reaction to proposals for greater Western European defense efforts and Moscow's apparent concern that the Eurogroup* in NATO may foreshadow increased Western European political cooperation, perhaps leading to a nuclear role for West Germany. Soviet comment suggests that nothing would be less desirable than a blend of "Europeanism" and "Atlanticism," which would stiffen the anti-Soviet political front in Europe all along the line.[41]

That, at least, is the argument; but it should be placed in a broader context. First of all, these Soviet expressions of concern may not reflect the thinking of the entire leadership. Although some Soviet leaders indeed may have many reasons to fear "the Europeanization of the cold war"—that is, some shift of the Western defense burden from the United States to Europe, perhaps including West German access to nuclear weapons—others may look on such a development in a different and more optimistic light. They may rely on Soviet diplomacy to undermine the rationale for a greater Western European defense

---

* Defense ministers of European NATO governments who meet periodically in an attempt to achieve consensus or compromise on NATO problems.

effort and closer Western European political ties. Even Soviet analyses that evoke the specter of a militarily strong and politically integrated Western Europe are often tempered by this consideration. In other words, Moscow deplores the prospect of an integrated Western Europe but considers it highly improbable. Thus, any change in the European-American relationship is normally seen by Moscow as both a challenge and an opportunity. The challenge is that this relationship may be placed on a more enduring basis; the opportunity points toward a Europe increasingly shorn of American influence and so riven by particularistic national interests as to become an inviting target for Soviet pressure.

Given this range of considerations, what policies is Moscow likely to pursue in the event of a unilateral reduction of American forces? In the short run, any such cut would be unlikely to produce a major change in Soviet policy, unless German reactions (discussed below) followed lines that created attractive opportunities. Moscow would be reluctant to risk catalyzing a combination of Western European defense cooperation and improved Atlantic coordination by increased threats and pressure. Still, if the danger of immediate destabilizing Soviet actions would be small, it must be added that desirable Soviet reactions would be equally unlikely to follow a cut in European-based U.S. forces.

A unilateral reduction of American forces would almost certainly rob the Soviet Union of any real incentive to negotiate a mutual and balanced reduction of forces on the Continent. Although Moscow has now shown public interest in mutual reductions, it is still hard to imagine the Soviet Union negotiating seriously if U.S. troops were withdrawn beforehand. Indeed, serious MBFR negotiations may well hinge on whether Moscow believes that the present U.S. commitment to maintain troop levels pending a successful outcome of the negotiations is something less than a firm commitment to maintain U.S. troop strength if the negotiations fail. Quite clearly, any mutual reduction of forces, however modest, will require hard diplomatic bargaining. It seems fanciful to assume that if the United States cut its forces unilaterally, the USSR would bypass negotiations in order to follow suit.

An incentive for reactive Soviet cuts in Europe might arise from a deepening of the Sino-Soviet conflict and a corollary need for additional troop concentrations on the Chinese border. But increased tension with China is not necessarily in the cards, and to transfer Soviet troops from Europe to Asia might undermine rather than buttress current Soviet efforts to improve relations with China. Moreover, should these efforts meet some success, the value Moscow attaches to a relaxation of tensions in Europe could easily diminish.

Finally, one should not lose sight of the police function of Soviet forces in Eastern Europe or their role in supporting Soviet claims to being a major European power. Instead of assuming that a unilateral cut in U.S. forces in Europe would be followed by a similar Soviet move, it is at least as plausible to view the former as a disincentive to the latter. Not only would Moscow be likely to fear the disruptive consequences of reducing Soviet forces in Eastern Europe, but Soviet leaders might find the prospect of an automatically improved military position vis-à-vis Western Europe too attractive politically to forgo.

None of these considerations is likely to be affected by the SALT negotiations, whatever their outcome. A SALT agreement would be viewed as confirming Soviet strategic parity with the United States; it would not cause Moscow to set less political store on its conventional forces in Europe. On the other hand, failure to reach agreement could sharpen the great-power rivalry and thus stimulate Soviet efforts to disengage Western Europe from the United States. Once again, undiminished Soviet military strength in Eastern Europe might appear to be a political asset of undiminished value.[42]

In estimating longer-term trends in Soviet policy that might follow U.S. troop reductions, special account should be taken of the likely German reaction. The Federal Republic's Ostpolitik relies on a strong Western alliance; Bonn strenuously opposes the idea of unilateral American troop withdrawals from Europe, arguing that it would be difficult to replace American with German forces—and that in any case a more national policy of deterrence "would lack both credibility and effectiveness."[43] Bonn frankly fears that American withdrawals would begin by undermining the Federal Republic's negotiating base in Eastern Europe and end by effecting a major political reorientation in Western Europe.

Such thinking carries a risk of self-fulfilling prophecy. Any weakening of Bonn's confidence in Washington seems almost certain to increase Soviet pressure on West Germany, a move that would reassure the East German regime, for which Bonn's Ostpolitik is a source of deep concern. The process could begin with renewed Soviet pressure on Berlin, despite the 1971 agreement regarding that city. The Kremlin might also adopt tactics of intimidation against Bonn that would go well beyond withdrawing earlier Soviet promises. The aim would be to extract further West German concessions, with the object of demoralizing West German political life and of weakening the Federal Republic's ties to the West. This would be all the more likely if, as seems probable for reasons discussed in Chapter 4, a unilateral U.S. troop reduction led not to a greater Western European defense effort, but rather to a general slackening of Western defense.

Here, too, the weakest link might well be the Federal Republic, where both official and popular attitudes strongly suggest that a U.S. decision to withdraw troops would be followed by cuts in the German armed forces. Even assuming that Moscow may not now be actively seeking to overturn the East-West balance in Europe, the emergence of a militarily weak, psychologically disoriented, and politically disarmed West Germany would strongly attract the Soviet Union toward a policy of renewed pressure on Western Europe.

Effects of Maintaining U.S. Force Levels

If the current American troop strength is maintained and the U.S. commitment to defend Western Europe remains credible to Moscow, Soviet policy will probably continue much as it is, with efforts to gain political influence in Western Europe through a policy of détente going hand in hand with measures to consolidate the Soviet position in Eastern Europe. If, over time, the Soviet government perceived a conflict between these purposes, it would undoubtedly give first priority to maintaining its grip on Eastern Europe. For example, if Chancellor Brandt's Ostpolitik threatened to produce change in Eastern Europe and especially East Germany, the Soviet Union would rapidly discard much of its present German policy.

None of this, however, need cause a return to the harsh bipolar confrontation of the cold war. While the prospects for a general political settlement that would substantially alter the status quo in Europe remain dim—they depend in part on the Soviet position elsewhere in the world, especially with regard to China—certain mutually acceptable steps to reduce the risks attendant on the present situation might become possible, such as the Berlin agreement. Moscow might even consider seriously the economic as well as political advantages to be gained by stabilizing the situation at a lower level of conventional military force through reciprocal force reductions in Europe.

Mutual force reductions might in turn produce further change. Some East-West arrangements would be needed to police and review these reductions on a continuing basis; these arrangements could bring together the United States, Western Europe, Eastern Europe, and the USSR in consultation and joint action on matters of common interest. The Soviet Union is not a monolithic entity; it is a multifaceted society facing major challenges, and it seems reasonable to believe that various groups within that society have differing views on policy toward the West. To the extent that East-West cooperation became a rewarding and continuing reality, even on a limited scale, those groups that favor a more relaxed policy might be marginally encouraged. The effect on the attitudes of groups in Eastern Europe might be more substantial, but therein lies a danger: The troop reductions might encourage Eastern European demands for greater freedom, bringing violent Soviet repression in return.

All of this hinges to some extent on the size of the mutual withdrawals. Relatively small reductions (say, about 10 percent) would not have a large early impact on either the Soviet Union or Eastern Europe, though they might have some useful long-term effect. Larger mutual reductions would have more substantial early effects, but larger reductions seem unlikely—even if U.S. forces are maintained at present levels—because of Soviet anxieties with respect to Eastern Europe. No East-West agreement or détente could give the Soviet Union the power it wants and now possesses, through its extensive Eastern European troop deployments, to arrest the processes of domestic change in individual Eastern European countries. It will take a long time for Soviet leaders to redefine their security interests in Eastern Europe in ways that would encourage a substantial (as distinct from symbolic) reduction of their forces, which might seem to place that power in jeopardy.

In sum, we seem to be facing what an astute European analyst has described as a " 'mixed-motive' Europe of 'imperfect partnership' and 'incomplete antagonism,' of overlapping groupings and cross-cutting alignments, of spectacular but inconsequential manoeuvres, of subterranean but essential evolution."[44] Whatever the shadings and fresh subtleties, the East-West environment is such that Europe's stability depends, much as before, on the larger system of global bipolarity. It thus presupposes a crucial role for the United States. It is true, of course, that future Soviet conduct in choosing between a more or a less constructive role in Europe will depend on many variables, only some of which can be influenced or controlled by the United States. Among these, the level of American forces on the Continent will be among the most significant.

3

The Military Balance

THROUGHOUT the 1950s and early 1960s, U.S. nuclear superiority in quality and quantity was said to serve as the umbrella for European security. The Soviet Union's buildup of its strategic posture was paralleled by a conscious American deceleration. Thus the 1970s opened in the context of nuclear parity—or stalemate—symbolized by the strategic arms limitation talks (SALT).

As SALT began, the incremental value of enlarging both offensive and defensive[1] strategic nuclear forces was believed to be small, given their large economic cost and the ease with which the other side could redress an imbalance. Thus the United States and the Soviet Union—and, with only minor misgivings, the major allies of both—came to accept the desirability of stabilizing nuclear forces at about the present level. An agreement to this effect is a possible though by no means assured outcome of SALT.[2]

Whether there is a military balance in Europe therefore depends not only on assessments of NATO and Warsaw Pact nuclear and conventional forces, but on how one views the relationship between nuclear and conventional forces in an era of East-West nuclear parity.

The Nuclear Equation

What, then, is the role of nuclear weapons—strategic and tactical—in the defense of Western Europe? One need not explore technical details or make precise calculations to conclude that the U.S. and Soviet strategic forces are in rough parity.[3] Regardless of the outcome of SALT, it is now officially conceded that neither side's nuclear arsenal can be used to coerce the other side to act contrary to its vital interests. This is so because the consequences for one superpower of having its bluff called successfully are exceeded only by the consequences for both sides of a nuclear threat carried out. This does not mean that nuclear weapons do not deter; rather, the significance of intercontinental nuclear parity is that deterrence is "mutual" at the level of a *strategic* exchange between the superpowers.

For Western Europe, this parity means that a "trip wire" strategy —which would automatically and immediately trigger the Western nuclear deterrent—has lost whatever validity it might theoretically have had during the period of American strategic nuclear superiority. (Paradoxically, even when the United States had superiority, it maintained more rather than fewer conventional forces in Europe than at present.[4]) Accordingly, the current and future relevance of strategic forces to Western European defense might be summarized as follows: Neither superpower will deliberately initiate a course of action that it believes could set in motion events that could lead to a strategic nuclear exchange.

What is inherently incredible as a peacetime proposition—for example, that either side would be willing to trade several (let alone most) of its major cities in trying to defend, say, its interests in Berlin—might be less incredible once the military forces of both superpowers were engaged in actual combat. At that point, the uncertainty compounded of irrationality, accident, miscalculation, and deliberate nuclear escalation would become a crucial factor, albeit one that cannot be reliably assessed. Therefore the role of nonnuclear forces in Central Europe is to deter the Warsaw Pact from employing military force against NATO and, in the event of conflict, to create the likelihood that nonnuclear combat will be sufficiently intense and prolonged to allow the nuclear powers (1) an opportunity to work out a diplomatic solution to the cause of hostilities and (2) time to take a measured decision regarding the use or non-use of nuclear weapons, rather than being forced to use them as a result of military weakness.

In this context, the term "tactical" is somewhat ambiguous when applied to nuclear weapons. What is "tactical" for the United States may well be "strategic" for Europeans living in the area of a nuclear detonation. Probably as good a working rule as any is to designate weapons as "intercontinental" and "theater," with a further stipulation that tactical theater weapons are those designed to influence the land or air defense battle *directly*, rather than indirectly (for example, by interdicting an enemy's lines of communication or by carrying a threat to his homeland).

The idea that tactical nuclear weapons furnish a plausible "option" for *defending* Western Europe (as distinguished from their escalatory role) has had a lingering half-life. In fact, the use of hundreds of atomic weapons could cause so much collateral damage to the area being "defended" that the inhabitants might prefer surrender as a lesser evil. This would be less true of certain low-yield or "clean" weapons; but even if NATO so limited its weaponry, an enemy might not.

The use of these weapons in Europe evokes a potential conflict of perceived interest between elements of the attentive publics in Europe and the United States. As Harlan Cleveland, a former U.S. ambassador to NATO, expressed it:

It is natural for Europeans to feel that if conventional defense fails in Europe, the use of nuclear weapons by NATO should rapidly escalate to a strategic exchange between the U.S. and Russia, leaving Europe comparatively intact. It is natural for Americans to press for effective, which is to say large-scale, use of nuclear weapons on the battlefield—enough to "stop the enemy in his tracks." But this conjures up for Europeans the picture of a Europe devastated while the United States and the Soviet Union remain intact.[5]

Nevertheless, according to news reports, the NATO Nuclear Planning Group has been making progress toward defining a number of hypothetical tactical nuclear options for NATO.[6] Paradoxical though it may seem, these options may give nuclear weapons a deterrent role to play. For the very existence of the options compels an enemy to disperse his offensive forces in order to reduce their vulnerability, thus countering the basic principle of massing for an attack. Even the possibility of tactical use therefore strengthens the deterrent. Their actual use, however, would raise enormously complex questions.

Some specialists contend that a controlled and discriminate use of low-yield tactical nuclear weapons could be managed without causing unacceptable collateral damage. Others, including a majority of responsible civilian leaders, believe otherwise. The ultimate military consequences of initiating the limited use of tactical nuclear weapons for defense against a conventional attack are essentially indeterminate, but the political impact could be enormous. An aggressor might react rashly and dangerously, but he would be in a dilemma if the defender limited the use of nuclear weapons to his own territory. If the aggressor chose to reply in kind, he would risk initiating an exchange of tactical nuclear weapons across international boundaries and in turn the ultimate disaster—a strategic exchange. But if he refrained from using his nuclear weapons, the defender might gain a significant advantage from unilateral defensive use—if in the process he did not cause unacceptable damage to his own territory.[7]

The trouble with this kind of analysis is that it assumes a degree of calmness and rationality that would almost certainly be absent once nuclear weapons began to be used. The only certainty is the danger that events would march in a direction foreseen by no one. For this and other reasons, the detonation of the first nuclear weapon to be used in anger since Hiroshima would mark a critical boundary. As former Secretary of Defense Robert McNamara said nearly a decade ago, "While it does not necessarily follow that the use of tactical nuclear weapons must inevitably escalate into global nuclear war, it does present a very definite threshold beyond which we enter a vast unknown."[8]

Thus the most that can be said of the tactical nuclear weapons now in Europe is that they may strengthen the deterrent by providing an ostensible link between employable military power—that is, conventional armaments—and the otherwise incredible use of strategic nuclear forces. Whether the existing number of weapons and systems on the Continent exceeds the requirement for this purpose (as at least two secretaries of defense came to believe) will not be analyzed here.

The United States has more than 7,000 tactical warheads in Europe, about three for each delivery system; the comparable Soviet figure is reported to be about 3,500 warheads.[9]

In sum, the possibility of nuclear escalation contributes importantly to the Western deterrent to all-out Soviet attack in present circumstances, and tactical nuclear weapons help to strengthen this option in some degree. Taking into account the possibility of loss through destruction, or unavailability in the confusion of battle, it is clear that NATO requires more than "a few" weapons to create this option. The number might well run into the thousands, given the size of the Soviet arsenal, which includes hundreds of medium-range ballistic missiles (MRBMs) as well as other tactical nuclear systems. Even so, it might be possible to reduce the present level, which was arrived at not by calculation but as an arbitrary cut-off point imposed by the Johnson administration. (The original stockpile of U.S. tactical nuclear warheads in Europe was presumably determined by resupply and rate-of-fire factors for the delivery systems then in or planned for Europe, at a time when tactical nuclear weapons were widely viewed as an appropriate means of compensating for deficiencies in conventional forces—hence simply as more powerful artillery.[10])

Whatever may be the most sensible view of tactical nuclear weapons, there are no ready tradeoffs between them and conventional forces. A credible tactical nuclear option, even for deterrence, may require more rather than fewer conventional forces in order to develop battlefield situations in which the use of these weapons would be relevant—in other words, to compel the enemy to mass his forces into suitable targets. Furthermore, an inadequate conventional force posture risks creating a situation in which tactical nuclear weapons would have to be used prematurely if they were used at all—to avoid either their loss or a military decision that would render their use irrelevant.

This discussion of strategic and tactical nuclear weapons points to the fact that conventional forces are the sine qua non for deterrence. For it is NATO's ability to engage any attacker, and to sustain combat for a substantial period of time *without* nuclear weapons, that makes the strategic deterrent and the potential tactical nuclear link to that deterrent credible.

The same reasoning could lead to a somewhat different conclusion—that given the unpredictable but certainly dire consequences of tactical nuclear defense and escalation, NATO's best option is to maximize its conventional force in order to make an attack so costly as to deter conventional actions and to rely on its nuclear arsenal solely to deter the other side from using nuclear weapons.[11] This was the burden of the U.S. policy message to Western Europe in the 1960s, when Washington urged its NATO partners to improve their forces. These exhortations aroused little response; though it was militarily and economically feasible, our emphasis on nonnuclear capabilities failed politically. Whereas Americans stressed the need for a "fighting" capability as a key ingredient of deterrence, the Western Europeans tended to look on deterrence as a more subtle equation and to give greater weight to the intentions than to the capabilities of the Warsaw Pact.

The Nature of the Threat

Both intentions and capabilities are involved, for a "threat" is the product of capabilities joined to intentions. For example, the enormous military superiority of the United States over, say, Mexico or Canada, is not perceived as a military threat in those countries, because there are no matching intentions to use that military force. Conversely, the much smaller Arab and Israeli capabilities are threats one to the other because of demonstrated intentions to employ them.

The threat to NATO clearly falls between the extremes. Soviet military capabilities are substantial and cover the spectrum of nuclear and nonnuclear contingencies.[12] They appear to some Western observers to be larger than would be called for by a noncommunist definition of requirements for defense and internal security; however, as former Ambassador George F. Kennan has pointed out, Russia has a tradition of large standing armies dating to precommunist times.[13]

Moreover, Soviet deployments in Eastern and Central Europe serve an obvious intrabloc security requirement.

All that can be said of Soviet intentions is that they are a compound not just of unknowns but of unknowables. The chief reason for the failure of Washington's plea for larger Western European defense efforts during the sixties is that the publics concerned—and their parliamentary representatives—simply do not believe that the Soviet Union is likely to use military force directly against the West. In short, the Warsaw Pact's impressive military capabilities are discounted by what are believed to be deterred (though not necessarily benign) intentions on the part of the present Soviet leaders.

On the other hand, Europe offers several examples of ways in which Soviet military power can be used to influence the political behavior of other states. Finland is an independent country, but it lives very much under the shadow of Soviet dominance and with constraints, which are nonetheless real for being subtle, on the conduct of its internal and external policies. And in Czechoslovakia, the world was put on notice that within the "socialist commonwealth," as Chairman Brezhnev called it, the Soviet Union will use whatever force it deems necessary to prevent what it regards as threatening political developments.[14]

Despite the renunciation of force in the Soviet-West German treaty of August 12, 1970 and in the September 1971 Berlin agreement, one can imagine circumstances in which Moscow might make a show of force along West Germany's borders or exert pressure on West Berlin's access routes in an effort to intimidate the Federal Republic. Indeed, this became a familiar pattern during the Berlin crises of the early sixties. And it is the possibility of large threatening maneuvers by Warsaw Pact forces, backed by political pressure on Berlin or elsewhere, that has produced allied agreement on the need to maintain a balance of conventional military forces in Europe. The U.S. role in this balance is particularly important; rightly or wrongly, Europeans believe that, as the December 1970 NATO ministerial communiqué put it, "substantial North American forces deployed in Europe [are] essential both politically and militarily.... Their replacement by European forces would be no substitute." Thus, recognition has grown that the political (or stability-building) functions of the military balance in Europe are as important as the classical military function.

The Opposing Conventional Forces

Maintenance of a politically stable balance of military forces in Europe serves three purposes:

First, it is essential for deterring all-out employment of the Warsaw Pact's conventional military resources against Western Europe—the least likely yet worst case, and one that NATO would have great difficulty countering. The NATO strategy of so-called flexible response, adopted in December 1967, is better described as deterrence by an *assured* response and a threat of "flexible" nuclear escalation, made credible by a conventional ability to prevent a sudden takeover by Pact forces.[15]

Second, it is needed to deal with other contingencies that could involve, either by design or by accident, the two Germanies, Berlin, or NATO's flanks, especially in the Mediterranean. Soviet restraint with respect either to accidental emergencies or to deliberately provoked crises would certainly depend in part on the overall East-West military balance and, most importantly, on the changed Soviet evaluation of *Western* intentions that might follow if NATO allowed its side of the balance to erode. The latter point is illustrated by a remark said to have been made by former Soviet Foreign Minister Molotov on U.S. behavior in Korea. He complained that when the United States withdrew from Korea in 1949–50, it did not leave behind so much as "a platoon with a flag" to show its concern; but when the North Koreans "sought to unify their country, America made a war out of it."[16]

Finally, the balance gives Europe confidence to build its own economic and political institutions and at the same time to reduce tensions between East and West. For example, the West Germans could hardly conduct their Ostpolitik if they could not rely on the Continent's political stability—a stability reinforced by the balance of conventional military force in Central Europe.

For these reasons, it is useful to outline the dimensions of the present balance. In so doing, three questions arise.

The first concerns the forces to be included. Should one count all the general purpose forces of NATO and the Warsaw Pact, including those of the United States and the Soviet Union, wherever deployed, or only those immediately available in the theater (which, for purposes of this discussion, means NATO's central region)? Obviously, neither extreme is satisfactory. One must begin with the immediately available forces deployed on both sides and add to them the reinforcements that could reasonably be expected at various periods of time.

The second, even more complex question is how to compare the military effectiveness of these forces.

Finally, one must ask what criteria should govern the comparison of opposing forces: the ability to deter, to contain, or to defeat an attack? And with what scenario in mind? A deliberate Soviet attack on Western Europe, planned to maximize surprise? A crisis that develops slowly, as over Berlin in 1961–62? An outbreak of violence in an Eastern European satellite, or some other unexpected contingency? A Soviet effort to intimidate West Germany or the Common Market?

Fundamental Positions

It is widely though wrongly believed that the public cannot reach sound judgments on issues like NATO defense because it lacks access to information that governments withhold for security reasons. A good deal of relevant information is highly classified, but the gap between open and secret data is greatly exaggerated. And the disparity is blurred by varying interpretations even of an agreed data base, both within governments and among scholars. Moreover, much classified information consists of technical details and qualitative appraisals that do not change the quantitative picture at the level of broad generalization.

The difficulty in assessing NATO's nonnuclear capabilities is not a lack of unclassified estimates, but the reverse. The public domain holds a wide variety of alternative estimates—by the U.S. Department of Defense, which tended during the 1960s to take a relatively hopeful view of NATO prospects; by NATO and other military authorities, who have tended toward a conservative (or pessimistic from NATO's standpoint) view of Soviet capabilities; and by the Institute for Strategic Studies (ISS) in London, whose efforts over the past decade are partly responsible for keeping the information gap so narrow, and whose views fall somewhere in the middle. Because it would be a book-length project to unravel the assumptions behind these conflicting estimates, it seems best for the purposes of this chapter to proceed from the ISS data, adjusted where necessary to take account of different assessments by others.[17] The discussion also includes data from the congressional testimony of U.S. government officials.

Consider first the overall American and Soviet defense postures, leaving aside the strategic forces discussed earlier.

The United States, with a population of 205 million, will have an active armed force of around 2.5 million men at the end of fiscal 1972. About 1 million of these compose the U.S. Army, organized into about thirteen divisions plus supporting units, with some 11,000 light aircraft and helicopters. Army reserve and national guard units have nearly two-thirds of a million men organized into eight modernized divisions and supporting units. The Air Force has approximately 7,000 first-line tactical aircraft (in a total of more than 12,000, including reconnaissance, airlift, air defense, and strategic forces). Three Marine air wings are associated with the three active Marine divisions. The Navy has somewhat fewer than 700 ships of all types (not counting the Polaris submarine force), including 13 attack carriers, each with an air wing. The United States has been spending nearly $80 billion a year for national defense; but as the Vietnam war is steadily scaled down, this figure should decline substantially in constant dollars. On this basis the defense budget will drop from roughly 7 percent of gross national product (GNP) in fiscal 1972 to around 6 percent.

The Soviet Union has a population of 244 million, an estimated

GNP of $466 billion, a current defense expenditure estimated at $52 billion (about 10 percent of GNP),[18] about 3.3 million men under arms plus another quarter-million in paramilitary forces, and 2 million men in various reserve training programs. The Red Army of more than 2 million men is organized into some 157 divisions, less than two-thirds of which are at or near high levels of readiness; the latter are stationed in Eastern Europe and the western USSR. The Soviet Air Force totals more than 10,000 combat aircraft and has been improving its qualitative standards. The Soviet Navy, which has rapidly become the world's second largest combat fleet, includes some 900 surface ships plus more than 350 submarines of all types. Future trends are hard to estimate. Thus far there has been little hard evidence that the Russians will follow the American example and reduce their general purpose forces, but internal pressures to give higher priority to domestic needs might lead to some reductions in future years, if Sino-Soviet tensions permit.

To these global postures of the superpowers, the other members of the NATO alliance, including France, add to the Western forces nearly 3 million men under arms, 4,200 combat aircraft, and 1,300 ships of varying types and quality, while the Warsaw Pact adds about 1 million men, 2,300 combat aircraft, and some 400 ships to the potential strength of the East.

In sum, the active military forces of all the NATO countries total around 5.5 million compared with 4.2 million for the Warsaw Pact.[19] These figures are consistent with those used in 1968 by the U.S. Department of Defense, if allowance is made for more than a half-million American servicemen who were in Southeast Asia in that year.

The Question of Relevance: NATO's Central Region

These broad aggregates highlight the importance of the question posed earlier: Which forces should be counted in describing the military balance in Central Europe?

U.S. secretaries of defense have often stressed the favorable global balance in NATO discussions. European defense ministers, on the other hand, have replied that the Soviet Union deploys much of its power in or closer to Central Europe—in East Germany, for example, where it can more readily be reinforced. In contrast, many of NATO's potential military assets are scattered along the rim of Western Europe, in North America or, currently, in the Far East.

Accordingly, it is appropriate to start with the deployed "M-day" forces immediately available to both sides in Central Europe.* Even here, reliable and useful figures are hard to determine. The ISS has made an estimate for 1970–71, shown in Table 3-1.

This table includes the forces in Northern Europe, where NATO has few assets but where the Soviet Union deploys substantial forces in its northern military districts. Undoubtedly the latter could be used against NATO's center instead of in the Baltic region, though some would surely be held back to maintain pressure on the northern flank. Technically, the ISS is correct in excluding French forces, since former President Charles de Gaulle deliberately cast doubt on their automatic participation with NATO forces, and they are still not available to NATO commanders in peacetime although they do participate in allied exercises. If included, they would add two divisions and 40,000 combat troops to the NATO totals; and since the French Army has more than 300,000 men, the gross manning strengths of the two sides are more nearly equal than the table suggests.

The numbers of tanks shown in the table are also questionable, for the NATO total does not include some 5,000 tanks in the war materiel reserve, repair pipeline, and prepositioned for American reinforcements.[20] Nor do such tabular listings reveal that NATO—reflecting its defensive role—has 50 percent more antitank weapons than does the Pact, more vehicles and helicopters, and an equal number of artillery and mortar tubes.[21]

Vital qualitative aspects are also necessarily omitted from simple comparisons of numbers of divisions or of troops, which taken alone

---

* By convention among analysts, active armed forces are called "M-day" forces—in this case, the active armed forces immediately available to the commanders in peacetime in Central Europe—since they compose the base posture that would be augmented by reinforcements as part of a buildup beginning on "mobilization day."

TABLE 3-1. *Military Forces Available to NATO and Warsaw Pact Commanders in Peacetime, by Category and Region, 1970–71*

	Northern and Central Europe[a]			Southern Europe[b]		
		Warsaw Pact			Warsaw Pact	
Category	NATO	Total	USSR	NATO	Total	USSR
Ground forces (in division equivalents)						
Armored	8	31	19	6	12	3
Infantry (mechanized and airborne)	16	38	21	28	22	3
Total[c]	24	69	40	34	34	6
Combat and direct support troops (thousands)	580	900	585	525	370	75
Main battle tanks	5,500	14,000	8,000	2,100	5,000	1,400
Tactical aircraft						
Light bombers	16	240	200	0	30	30
Fighter/ground attack	1,400	1,300	1,000	600	200	50
Interceptors	350	2,000	900	250	850	450
Reconnaissance	400	400	300	100	100	40
Total[c]	2,166	3,940	2,400	950	1,180	570

Source: Adapted from *The Military Balance, 1970–71* (London: Institute for Strategic Studies, 1970), pp. 91–94.

a. Includes, on the NATO side, the commands for which AFCENT and AFNORTH are responsible; France is *not* included. On the Warsaw Pact side, includes the command for which the Pact High Commander has responsibility but excludes the armed forces of Bulgaria, Hungary, and Romania; Soviet units normally stationed in the western USSR and such troops as might be committed to the Baltic theater of operations have, however, been included.

b. Includes, on the NATO side, the Italian, Greek, and Turkish land forces and such U.S. and British units as would be committed to the Mediterranean theater of operations, and on the Pact side, the land forces of Bulgaria, Romania, and Hungary and such Soviet units normally stationed in Hungary and the southern USSR as might be committed to the Mediterranean theater.

c. Numbers of divisions and of tactical aircraft have been totaled for convenience, but totals should be used with caution.

can be a misleading measure of military power. As will be explained later, even the concept of the "division" or the "division slice" (which adds indirect support to the combat and direct support troops counted by the ISS) is misleading because of the different ways in which forces are organized and employed in NATO and the Warsaw Pact. One such count credits NATO (including France) with 677,000 men in division forces as against 619,000 for the Warsaw Pact,[22] many of whose divisions are kept below full strength and some of which would require major reinforcement before combat. It can be seen, therefore, that many Soviet divisions really serve the same purpose as the men and equipment in what NATO would call its "pipeline," rather than its order of battle.

The difficulties of compiling valid comparative data are especially great in the case of aircraft, since quality and performance are critical and many Soviet aircraft are designed for air defense rather than air superiority roles. Former Secretary of Defense McNamara said in his fiscal year 1969 posture statement: "In the case of air forces, our relative capability is far greater than a simple comparison of numbers would indicate. By almost every measure—range, payload, ordnance effectiveness, loiter time, crew training—NATO (especially U.S.) air forces are better than the Pact's for non-nuclear war...."[23]

Augmentation

Augmentation of the basic posture depends critically on assumptions about the timing of force buildups by the two alliances. Would both sides start simultaneously? Or would the Soviet Union, as in the case of Czechoslovakia, act first by bringing its units up to strength and moving them forward under the guise of maneuvers, before NATO reinforced its front-line forces?*

This problem of timing highlights the well-known geographic asymmetry that favors the Warsaw Pact and is reinforced by an assumed asymmetry of initiative. For even with maximum warning from intelligence sources, NATO would require considerable time to reach political decisions and react by moving its forces. Democracies in any case cannot mobilize rapidly unless they live in a constant state

---

* According to Harlan Cleveland, in 1968 NATO made a conscious decision not to mobilize (hence not to give the USSR an excuse for invading Czechoslovakia in order to "protect" it) because the buildup by the Warsaw Pact was clearly not directed against the West. Some 250,000 Pact troops in 25 divisions with their supporting aircraft were involved in staging this invasion, though not all of them entered Czechoslovakia. (See "NATO After the Invasion," *Foreign Affairs*, Vol. 48 [January 1969], p. 254.)

of alert, like Israel, or unless they have a tradition of citizen soldiers manning a small, highly defensible area, like Switzerland. This applies even more to a multinational alliance.

Reliable data on the reinforcement capabilities of NATO and the Warsaw Pact are not available in published sources.[24] Some general judgments were offered by former Secretary of Defense McNamara in his fiscal 1969 posture statement:

Assuming a simultaneous mobilization, within 30 days the Pact could probably gain a manpower advantage on the Central Front and a somewhat greater advantage in overall ground combat capability. This gap would then begin to narrow with the arrival of more U.S. forces.

NATO tactical aircraft reinforcements would about equal the Pact's in the early stages of mobilization, after which we could add considerably more aircraft than the Pact. Our main advantage in this area, however, stems from the great superiority of our aircraft, pilots and weapons....

The most likely kind of conflict in NATO Europe is one arising from miscalculation during a period of tension, rather than a deliberately preplanned Soviet attack. In this kind of crisis, the Soviets would not necessarily have the initiative in mobilizing and deploying troops. Even though the Pact forces could mobilize somewhat faster than NATO, they would not achieve a decisive advantage. Furthermore, NATO has an air advantage. It would thus appear that the balance of forces would, over time, be sufficient to cope with the situation. ...[25]

The ISS estimates of the military balance in 1970–71 are very specific. They suggest that within less than a month, the Soviet Union could bring most of its forward-deployed forces up to full strength in men and equipment and reinforce the 31 divisions now in Central Europe with up to 39 additional divisions (possibly using some from the northern region) for a total of 70. If all the divisions in East Germany, Poland, and Czechoslovakia were similarly brought up to high or full strength, and if they were considered available for the central region, then the Warsaw Pact force in this area could reach 103 divisions within thirty days after starting mobilization (M + 30). Much would depend on whether the Pact's logistic system could support these divisions; for the system is makeshift by NATO standards, often relying directly on civilian transport and maintenance.

The associated manpower figure for combat and direct support troops might be nearly 1.5 million men for the Pact if mobilization proceeded smoothly.[26] With respect to tanks, if the Soviet Union and its allies procured the total called for by their table of organization and equipment (325 vehicles for each tank division and 175 for each motorized rifle division), they would have an enormous inventory of more than 30,000 medium tanks. But such procurement levels seem doubtful, especially since one-third of the Pact divisions are maintained at considerably reduced levels of manning and, presumably, of equipment. Nevertheless, the M-day tank strength of 14,000 could probably be increased by at least one-half at M + 30, to more than 20,000 tanks for the Pact's 103 divisions.

On the NATO side, there would be little quantitative increase in forces during the first two weeks of a buildup, though front-line units could be brought to full readiness, the German territorial (supporting) troops mobilized, and a start made on troop and aircraft redeployment from the United States and the United Kingdom. However, a crisis grave enough to cause the West to mobilize would probably bring France back to full collaboration with its allies. If one adds the two French divisions now in Germany and one from France—plus some forces deployed from the United States, Britain, and Canada—then NATO's M + 30 strength might be thirty divisions in the center, assuming combat and direct support manpower of about 720,000 and a 24,000-man division combat and direct support "slice," as in Table 3-1. Some of the stockpiled tanks could also be activated, increasing NATO's active tank inventory to 7,000 or more. They would be augmented by many antitank weapons in both regular and militia-type forces.

NATO has the larger reserve of aircraft, since forward-deployed air forces represent only 20 percent of its worldwide inventory compared with 40 percent for the Pact.[27] But the Pact has a network of well-dispersed and well-defended airfields in Eastern Europe. NATO is handicapped by having access to fewer military airfields, even assuming the availability of French facilities, and by the transatlantic distances involved in resupply operations. If both sides could achieve

a 50 percent increase by M + 30—which would be doing well—
NATO would have a theater inventory of 3,000 or more aircraft
compared with as many as 6,000 tactical aircraft for the Pact.
NATO's aircraft, however, have at least twice the range, payload,
and loiter time of the Pact's and are generally more versatile.

Thus, in the short term, the Warsaw Pact can increase its forward-
deployed forces at a faster rate than NATO. Even if French forces
are included, the ratios of men, divisions, tanks, and aircraft worsen
for NATO in the central region between M-day and M + 30. The
foregoing approximations based on ISS data can be stated as ratios
between the NATO and Warsaw Pact forces:

	M-day (without France)	M + 30 (with France)
Ground force manpower	1:1.6	1:2.1
Divisions	1:2.9	1:3.4
Tanks	1:2.5	1:2.9
Tactical aircraft	1:1.8	1:2.0

These crude ratios omit some important qualitative factors and
could be misleading if taken by themselves. For instance, they assume a "pre-hostilities" environment for reinforcement. During actual combat, supply lines and bases could be attacked, logistics dis-
rupted, territory lost, and replacement units and stocks of equipment
destroyed. This might place additional handicaps on NATO because
of the geographic asymmetries of the two sides. On the other hand,
the Pact forces' lower standards of logistics and maintenance would
partially offset their geographic advantage. If the conflict reached the
level of thermonuclear exchange, the question of reinforcement would
of course be irrelevant.

Both the ISS and the Defense Department data suggest that if the
peak of the Warsaw Pact's superiority—reached, say, in twenty to
thirty days after it began augmentation—passed without an attack,
then the West could begin to improve its position against the East.
Over a still longer period, this process would continue as the stronger
mobilization base in the West began to have its effect. It can be as-

sumed that by M + 90, all twenty-eight continental NATO divisions (including the equivalent of eleven from France under full mobilization) would be at full strength. Britain, Canada, and the United States could contribute up to twenty-two divisions, with a maximum effort, making the NATO total fifty divisions;[28] but many military men question the quality of equipment and training of such units after only three months of mobilization.

The Warsaw Pact, on the other hand, might increase its M + 90 European theater force to about 150 divisions (out of its total force structure of 214 divisions).[29] The associated Pact manpower would be roughly 2.25 million men compared with more than 1 million for NATO.[30] The tank and aircraft holdings of both sides would also increase substantially, with NATO gaining relatively in aircraft and possibly losing in tanks. But the longer the mobilization continued, the more NATO could relieve its apparent inferiority in the M-day balance—assuming an all-out effort, full participation by France, and no active hostilities to interfere with the buildup.

Problems of Comparison

The raw data pose a second question: How does one compare forces in a useful fashion? Military forces do not equal military capabilities, for the latter also represent intangibles of leadership, training, morale, discipline, and organization. Moreover, capabilities are only putative, for history shows that the outcome of an engagement depends as much on surprise, terrain, weather (and its effect on air power)—and luck —as it does on the relative strength of the forces involved. The Germans, for example, undertook the Ardennes offensive in December 1944 against an overall Allied superiority of two to one, but they achieved at least an initial success by exploiting these factors.

Only if one hypothesized that other things are approximately equal and that a Warsaw Pact soldier is roughly equivalent to a NATO soldier, could one assume that the relative quantity of forces is a good indicator of capabilities in the abstract. But the vulnerability of this hypothesis (since other things rarely are equal) makes the assumption invalid. In the real world, capabilities are heavily dependent on the scenario and the qualitative factors just mentioned. For example, as noted below, the fact that most Eastern European forces could prove unreliable in many situations limits the value of quantitative comparisons that include them.

One should also adjust for the fact that while some of the greater costs of NATO (especially American) forces as compared to Warsaw Pact armies reflect higher pay, procurement costs, and living standards that might be called "fat," some of this surely buys greater combat effectiveness in weapons and equipment. In Europe, a typical Warsaw Pact formation (division or brigade) is only one-half to two-thirds as large as its NATO counterpart. NATO units are ahead, on the whole, in comparative firepower measurements, their greater number of antitank weapons partially offsetting the Pact's superiority in tanks. A Pact division therefore may be conservatively estimated as equivalent to about two-thirds of a NATO division, even without adjusting for the former's weaker supporting structure.[31]

This weaker supporting structure reflects a different philosophy regarding the use of divisions. A Soviet assault division is considered expendable; when casualties are such that it can no longer operate effectively, it is simply replaced by another unit. While this may make them cost-effective in an assault role, it limits the number of divisions that can be employed simultaneously in the battle area and makes it difficult to deduce Soviet combat strength from the total number of Soviet divisions on hand. In contrast, Western divisions are designed to be maintained as continuing combat entities; because they are resupplied, reequipped, and their casualties are replaced, their logistic "tails" are far larger—but provide greater staying power—than their Soviet counterparts.

Thus, numbers of divisions are as misleading as total manpower numbers as a basis for comparison. As was noted earlier, the Soviet Union maintains on paper a structure of nearly 160 divisions in an army of about 2 million men, while the United States currently has only about 13 division forces in an army of 1 million men. This reflects not only division "slices" of vastly different size and the differ-

ing approaches to battle employment and logistic support already
mentioned, but also the advantages of a contiguous over a far distant
theater.

The reliability of Eastern European units is another consideration.
Are they net additions to Soviet forces? Or, in an offensive operation,
would they be potential liabilities? In the latter case, would Soviet
planners deduct them from the order of battle and assume that they
would create a need for additional *Soviet* forces to maintain local control? While there is no definite answer, Soviet concern with this question seems likely to be greater in the confusion of sustained combat,
when disaffection could spread in Eastern Europe, than in an operation
that might be completed before opposition could be organized. Thus,
the larger are NATO's nonnuclear forces and defensive ability, the
more uncertain are the duration and outcome of an Eastern-instigated
conflict and the more the Soviet Union must worry about these reliability factors.

Criteria for Evaluation

Having considered what to count and how to compare what has
been counted, one is left with the third question: What are the criteria
for evaluating the European military balance? The main ones debated
during recent years are the defensive or "war-fighting" capability
(which has been a primary concern of the Pentagon) and the deterrence of aggression or its threat (on which Western Europeans have
concentrated, with a tendency to ignore what would happen "if deterrence fails"). The new NATO strategy adopted in December 1967 in
effect bridges this gap by making clear that credible deterrence depends on a substantial conventional combat capability.

There are those, however, who argue that a large-scale attack is
the wrong contingency against which to plan—or by which to judge
the stability of the conventional military balance—since it is the least
likely. They contend that the criterion should be an ability to handle
less unlikely developments, such as pressures on borders or corridors,
local hostilities, a renewed Berlin crisis, or a spillover from an upris-

ing in Eastern Europe. But Soviet restraint in such lesser cases—and the continued unlikelihood of major aggression (or its threat as a means of exerting political pressure)—may well depend on Moscow's assessment of the balance as it applies to major military conflicts. And, as was argued earlier, Western European confidence in a stable military balance may be essential for policies aimed at establishing a more viable relationship with the East.

The Balance in Perspective

The preceding discussion suggests that the quantitative nonnuclear balance, even measured in gross numbers, is not so adverse to NATO as has often been claimed, and is even less so when adjusted for qualitative factors. Conventional military wisdom suggests that a three-to-one superiority is required for a successful attack in a given area. NATO's inferiority in numbers of divisions would be of this magnitude only at the $M + 30$ stage of mobilization; even then it would fall to about two-to-one if adjusted for the size of the respective divisions and for qualitative factors. Nevertheless, those who attach heavy weight to geographic asymmetries, and to advantages of initiative and surprise that could allow the aggressor to attain more than a three-to-one ratio in a particular sector, tend to be pessimistic about the current military balance as measured by conventional combat capability.

Most experienced military officers would assert that the net preponderance of Warsaw Pact forces, coupled with an assumed initiative, affords the East a degree of superiority for a large-scale deliberate attack. This group can be divided into those who think the preponderance is such that nothing NATO could do within the present political-economic context could redress the conventional imbalance—hence that heavy reliance must be placed on nuclear weapons—and those who believe that a marginally greater and better-organized common defense effort could significantly improve the balance. The latter school emphasizes qualitative improvements in training, equipment, and supplies for the European forces, and in antitank and antiaircraft defenses. This group would also correct a long-standing maldeployment of American forces by moving them from Bavaria into the more critical North German plain. As a result of studies conducted during its first two years in office, the Nixon administration has apparently joined the school of thought that stresses qualitative improvement.[32]

A distinct minority are those who believe that a nonnuclear balance could be maintained even at a substantially lower level of Western (or American) effort than now exists.[33] These optimists and the pessimists who despair of redressing the imbalance sometimes reach similar conclusions by opposite routes, the former perceiving the present balance as permitting the West to reduce its effort, the latter considering it so inadequate as to make conventional forces irrelevant and hence unnecessary. If, the argument runs, Soviet forces could reach the Rhine in a few days or weeks anyway, why not let them get there twice as fast and save half the money?[34] Both arguments sustain budget cutters in NATO's parliaments.

Another view can be found between these extremes. It holds that a long period of mobilization before the outbreak of hostilities might enable the West to achieve a better balance with the Pact in usable military capability deployed to Central Europe; but that in a shorter mobilization period the East could achieve a significant superiority that might affect the political behavior of both sides, even if it were not employed militarily. Those who hold this view tend to favor the qualitative NATO improvements referred to earlier and to believe that their effect could be significant.

This summary of differing views does not automatically suggest an answer to the basic question: How stable is the present balance of military power? In a technical sense—that is, in judging how that balance could affect large-scale combat in event of war—the answer is probably unknowable; there are too many imponderables. But in a political sense—judging how the balance affects deterrence—a good deal of postwar experience is available for guidance. The existing balance has been consistent with effective deterrence for two decades.

This history reinforces the judgment, implicit in the foregoing analysis, that the risks and effects of the present nonnuclear balance in

Europe—even if it is somewhat unfavorable to NATO in quantitative military terms—are acceptable in current circumstances. This judgment takes deterrence as the chief criterion, while assuming that substantial combat capability is basic to deterrence.

Involved in this judgment, as in NATO's current strategy, is the assumption that since present Soviet intentions do not appear to be aggressive, shifts in the attitudes of the Warsaw Pact leaders, or major external developments affecting them, could be discerned before those intentions changed. This is not the same as "warning time" in the classical military sense; rather, it assumes that Soviet perceptions of the situation would change in a manner visible to the West, and that a significantly stronger probability of conflict would be detected in time to permit Western countermeasures and diplomatic crisis management—provided, of course, that the West was able to use that time to advantage.

In sum, it is reasonable to conclude that any current advantage to the Warsaw Pact in forces readily available in Central Europe is partially offset by other factors that favor the West. Even if there is not a "balance" in the narrowest military sense, there probably *is* a balance in the political-military context of deterrence. The "relation of forces" (as the Russians term it) seems to have deterred aggression and rebuffed pressure for twenty years. This affords grounds for hope that the existing political-military balance will continue to be effective—if it can be maintained.

NATO's Flanks and the Mediterranean

Thus far the analysis has treated the European security problem as though it concerned only one geographic region: Central Europe. In fact, although this is the most important zone from the standpoint of conflicting Western and Eastern interests (and is consequently where the bulk of U.S. forces are located), NATO consists of three essentially separate regions—northern, central, and southern—in addition to the area of the United Kingdom and the Channel, the Atlantic, and North America. In actual terrain, the central front covers only about

600 miles of NATO Europe's total eastern land frontier of approximately 5,300 miles.

To the north, the Kiel Canal links the North Sea to the Baltic and separates Central Europe from the narrow Danish peninsula and mountainous Norway. These northern NATO states undoubtedly consider their eastern Nordic neighbors, Sweden and Finland, as a nonaligned defensive buffer, even though this thousand-mile land barrier can be bypassed at sea.

To the south, the neutral territories of Austria and Switzerland project laterally across both sides of the north-south line that divides Europe, reaching eastward and westward far into the defended areas of the opposing alliances. They separate the German/Benelux heartland of the alliance from NATO's Mediterranean members: Italy, Greece, and Turkey. Thus, NATO's two northern and three southern members share a greater exposure to—and reliance on—adjacent seas and oceans, underscoring the need for naval forces to protect their shipping and sea frontiers. This seaborne emphasis in the southern region contrasts with the heavy concentration of ground forces and tactical air support in the center.

The mobility and availability of naval units complicates the problem of estimating the rough dimensions of the present conventional military balance on NATO's flanks, particularly with regard to the question of "what forces to count." Aside from small forces maintained by Norway and Denmark for coastal and territorial defense, and West Germany's Baltic fleet, NATO's northern region must rely primarily on substantial reinforcement in time of crisis. To the extent that this would involve adding external forces to units mobilized in Denmark and Norway, it would require substantial naval and air capabilities on the part of the other NATO allies. This becomes all the more important because of the disparity in M-day ground forces in the northern region, where Soviet combat manpower in nearby northwestern Russia outnumbers locally available NATO forces by as much as five to one. The "thin blue line" is at its thinnest in Norway and Denmark, where weather and geography complicate the reinforcement problem.

The defense problem for NATO's southern member states is complicated by political-military factors. Among these are the proximity of the Middle Eastern tinderbox, the Greek-Turkish dispute over Cyprus, the unpopularity of the military government in Greece elsewhere in NATO, and the USSR's increased naval capability and influence along the Arab littoral of the Mediterranean. In addition to possible pressure on the borders of Thrace and eastern Turkey, NATO's southern region faces a continuing possibility of Arab-Israeli conflict in the Middle East and increased naval vulnerability in the Mediterranean. In a war at sea, however, the present U.S. Sixth Fleet would be more than a match for the Soviet Mediterranean squadron (unless it were caught by a sneak attack), and the French and Italian naval forces in the Mediterranean are each as strong as the Soviet fleet deployed there. Nonetheless, the Russian fleet complicates NATO defense plans and enhances Soviet diplomacy.[35]

At a superficial glance, the conventional military balance in Southeastern Europe as shown in Table 3-1 might seem to favor NATO in M-day ground force divisions, combat manpower, and tactical air capabilities (if not in numbers of aircraft), though the Warsaw Pact tank force outnumbers NATO's here, as in Central Europe. But the comparison is misleading in that it counts Italian forces as part of NATO's military capability to defend the southern region. The most likely areas of tension are not the westward invasion routes, where Italian forces might come into play, but rather Greek and Turkish Thrace and eastern Turkey—defensive zones remote from the Italian peninsula, with distant reinforcement susceptible to Soviet interdiction at sea and in the air. When discounted for this factor—and after making a similar adjustment for Hungary on the other side—the southeastern balance of nonnuclear M-day forces is not so uneven in gross terms. But this conclusion depends critically on the number of Soviet forces that are included. The ISS counts only six Soviet divisions in the Warsaw Pact's southeastern order of battle, though twenty-eight divisions—many of them understrength—are potentially available in the adjacent regions of Russia.

As in the central region, the Pact enjoys a short-term advantage over the West in augmenting its forces, primarily because NATO must reinforce its isolated flanks by sea and air over long distances, while the Pact can more rapidly augment its forward positions using high-capacity land transport in the southern USSR, Romania, and Bulgaria. Even if this short-term imbalance were partly offset by the timely arrival of American units, the Pact might already have achieved objectives such as overrunning the narrow defense perimeter of Thrace or seizing the Turkish straits. Moreover, augmentation assumes a ready source of reinforcements; but NATO military commanders point out that a major crisis on NATO's flanks would hardly be the time to weaken the alliance's defense posture in Central Europe by moving units away from this area. Thus the major contribution would have to come from "external" forces, for example in Britain and North America, which would take time to arrive. Reinforcement from Italy would encounter political obstacles in that country as well as the logistic difficulties noted earlier.

Nevertheless, NATO has taken a number of defensive measures to assure the immediate involvement, at least symbolically, of other members of the alliance in the event of conflict or critical tensions on its flanks. The most widely publicized has been the active exercising since 1962 of the Allied Command Europe Mobile Force (AMF), consisting of a multinational airborne brigade with tactical air support. Eight member nations contribute to battalion-sized units that are on call for use with a squadron of aircraft from five allies.[36] Similarly, internationally integrated naval forces are operating in the Atlantic (the Standing Naval Force, Atlantic, or STANAVFORLANT, from seven nations) and in the Mediterranean (the On-Call Naval Force, Mediterranean, or NAVOCFORMED, from six or seven nations). And a special air surveillance unit—the Maritime Air Force, Mediterranean (MARAIRMED)—composed of British, American, Italian, and French land-based patrol aircraft, provides reports on Soviet Mediterranean fleet operations. Thus the capability exists for forcefully demonstrating NATO solidarity in the event of Warsaw Pact pressure on NATO's flanks.

However, it should be noted that a vital contributor to flank reinforcement, the U.S. Sixth Fleet, has another important role in stabilizing the precarious balance in the Middle East. This fleet is a NATO force only when placed in the alliance chain of command; neither these American naval units in the Mediterranean nor their counterpart in American home waters, the U.S. Second Fleet (which is also responsible for meeting contingencies in the North and South Atlantic), can be considered purely in the NATO context. Indeed, given the high level of tension in the Arab-Israeli conflict since the June 1967 war, it might be said that the major purpose of the U.S. Sixth Fleet is peacekeeping in the Middle East and the Mediterranean area generally. The Sixth Fleet is also a significant element in U.S. military relations with Spain, whose future is an important factor in European as well as Mediterranean security, and an anchor for Spain's own sense of security, which in turn may improve the prospects for political liberalization.

In summary, NATO's flanks remain vulnerable to Soviet political-military pressure. Mutual force reductions, discussed below, are even harder to envisage in the flanks than in the center, except possibly for bilateral efforts involving Greece or Turkey and Bulgaria or Romania. As for unilateral American reductions, the only sizable U.S. force in the area is the Sixth Fleet, which currently maintains two carrier task forces on station backed by four in the Second Fleet. Eliminating one of these six task forces may be manageable, if the Navy can improve on its practice of maintaining two back-up carriers for each carrier on station. The pros and cons of this change involve highly technical questions of maintenance, personnel, and logistics that exceed the scope of this study.

Mutual Force Reductions

There is a long history of postwar schemes for disengagement, disarmament, and arms control in Central Europe.[37] Mutual and balanced force reductions (MBFR) between NATO and the Warsaw Pact have been in vogue conversationally during the last three years, yet their substance is extraordinarily complicated—even more so than that of SALT. For Soviet forces in Eastern Europe meet an internal security need in addition to balancing Western forces in NATO.

Moreover, the different geostrategic positions of the USSR and NATO add to the difficulties of comparing the two different force structures. Nevertheless, as is noted in Chapters 2 and 6, the MBFR issue is moving toward center stage, with negotiations a lively possibility; and it seems important to encourage the start of a process that might lead eventually to reductions by both sides, implemented in stages after appropriate verification.[38]

Given the rather precarious military balance in Central Europe, purely symmetrical reductions (say, in percentages) might not be in NATO's interest even though the Soviets, having larger forces, would withdraw more men. For while the residual force ratios might be unchanged, NATO's capability might be reduced below a viable minimum, depending on the percentage of reduction. And any U.S. forces withdrawn would be moved back thousands of miles in contrast to Soviet forces, which would remain nearby. Furthermore, with respect to deactivated manpower, the Soviet mobilization system is probably more efficient, and certainly more reliable from a military commander's point of view, than any Western counterpart.

NATO therefore might be compelled to seek unequal reductions, either by attempting to reach a "man-to-mile equivalency" in forces withdrawn—that is, 1,000 men withdrawn 3,000 miles might require, say, 6,000 men as a counter if the latter were withdrawn only 500 miles—or by some other formula. Or part of the offset to reduction of certain Soviet forces in Eastern Europe might be provided by nonequivalent NATO reductions—for example, in the Sixth Fleet in the Mediterranean or in nuclear systems that may exceed NATO's minimum needs. Within NATO, however, trading, say, an American cutback in the Mediterranean for a Soviet ground force reduction in East Germany would be politically difficult, since some members of the alliance would gain while others would be exposed to increased risks.

Unilateral Reductions

The next question—which is critical in the context of this study—is what unilateral changes, if any, the West could afford to make in its nonnuclear defense posture without causing either damaging political repercussions or a noticeable shift in the military balance. A commonsense if somewhat intuitive judgment is that Western force reductions of 20 percent or more could affect capability sufficiently to tilt the balance, whereas much smaller adjustments, say 5 to 10 percent, might not. The range between must be considered an open question whose answer depends largely on the sensitivity of the balance— that is, on the perceptions of political leaders on both sides. It should be understood that as East-West parity in strategic nuclear forces is generally recognized, the sensitivity of the nonnuclear balance is increased.

One way to test this intuitive judgment is to ask how unilateral cuts in U.S. troop deployments, if they became necessary, might be achieved with least damage to the alliance. This would pose three broad issues for U.S. military policy (the political implications are discussed in Chapter 4):

1. Should all (or substantially all) of the U.S. combat forces in the European theater be retained while headquarters and support activities are reduced? Or should combat forces be reduced and the support structure required for the rapid return of withdrawn units be kept intact?

2. Should a reduction be concentrated in a single element—the ground, air, or naval forces—or should across-the-board cuts be made in the forces deployed by all three services?

3. Should American forces in Europe be restructured—recognizing, of course, that this would affect the strategy and forces of the alliance as a whole, at least in the center—or should the existing structure and missions be retained but at lower levels of manning?

These issues are considered in turn.

Combat versus support. The present level of approximately 300,000 men reflects a cut of more than 25 percent from the postwar peak in the 1960s. It was achieved by substantially reducing headquarters and support activities and by redeploying 35,000 men in 1968 as part of a "dual basing" agreement in NATO. This process has probably left little "fat" to cut, as opposed to "bone and muscle." Several programs for streamlining support and overhead activities and for combining headquarters have come forward and have attracted considerable congressional interest.[39] Savings realizable without harmful effects obviously should be made, but the scope for major personnel reductions through these programs appears to be small.

As noted, the military balance depends in part on NATO's ability to augment its peacetime forces in the event of a renewed crisis. The American force structure in Europe has been designed for augmentation; further reductions in service and support units or personnel would lengthen the delay before combat reinforcements could be received and made operational in Europe, curtailing the American forces' ability to maintain sustained combat. (Supplies for sixty to ninety days of combat are currently stockpiled.)

Thus, reducing the U.S. support element might create a posture that was essentially "all teeth and no tail." This force might have an impressive fighting capability for a short time—probably as long as most of our allies could fight on the central front—but it could not be rapidly reinforced, leaving substantial American forces in a highly vulnerable military position.

Shifting to a "short war" strategy would also have an adverse psychological effect in Western Europe. It is the known reinforcement and augmentation potential from the United States that redresses NATO's somewhat adverse peacetime balance of forces in the Europeans' view; reducing that potential could be prejudicial to their confidence in the Western position. While savings might be achieved by reducing the resupply requirement—and thus the expensive antisubmarine forces maintained to guard lines of communication to Europe—the deterrent effect of a "finite" American commitment undoubtedly would be less convincing. The present commitment, being continuous, links NATO to the economic power of the United States. Weakening this link could affect not only Western attitudes but also deterrence vis-à-vis the Soviet Union.

A further drawback is that any reduction in NATO's conventional combat capability risks creating pressures for early use of tactical nuclear weapons. Such a reduction therefore might confront NATO with the most intractable political issues relating to control of nuclear weapons in peacetime consultations, or early in the transition from peace to war. It might lead the European governments to grapple with questions regarding the creation of a European nuclear deterrent before they were politically able to resolve them, with consequent divisive effects in the alliance.

The merit of the reverse option—"more tail than teeth"—is that combat forces can be moved more rapidly than combat support, especially as the giant C-5A transport comes into use. But this option too has disadvantages: should deterrence fail, NATO's ability to hold, pending reinforcement, would be reduced. And it is combat rather than supporting forces that provide the political impact of the American presence, in the view of both our European allies and the Soviet Union.

Across-the-board versus single-service cuts. The Navy is an obvious target for single-service reductions because of its marginal influence on the land battle in the center. In part this involves considerations of geography as well as service—that is, the relative priority of the Mediterranean and the center. But it also involves technical issues: Although naval forces are critical in safeguarding lines of communication and in reinforcing both of NATO's flanks, a case can be made, as indicated earlier, for reducing by one the carrier task forces assigned to the Second Fleet in the Atlantic and/or the Sixth Fleet in the Mediterranean. (On the other hand, such savings as are possible in carrier task forces might as easily be made in the Pacific when the force reduction in Vietnam permits.[40])

The arguments are more complex with regard to concentrating reductions in the air or ground forces. The greater relative mobility of air power argues for redeploying additional aircraft from Europe to the United States; but four tactical fighter squadrons are already "dual based," and if the United States were to move further toward relying on reinforcement under combat conditions, the resulting impairment of the M-day air power balance might mean that NATO would have too few or no airfields on which to land. On the other hand, concentrating reductions in ground forces might place too much of the initial defense burden on air power, which can be highly sensitive to weather. Moreover, ground divisions contribute more than air forces to supporting deterrence and to maintaining allied confidence. Thus, posing the question of troop versus air reductions presents the military planner with Hobson's choice.

Restructuring versus thinning out. Given the difficulty of choosing between cuts in combat forces as against supporting units, or across-the-board rather than in a single service, military planners might prefer to examine other alternatives. Manning levels could of course be reduced without withdrawing any units as such; but this would impair the readiness of forces up and down the line and would contravene NATO standards on which the United States has always insisted. Therefore, restructuring might be considered preferable.

One way would be to redistribute NATO resources among the four separate elements of ground forces. These elements consist of (1) forward-defense units, whose screening and covering function helps to identify an attack and compels an enemy to mass his forces; (2) main maneuver forces, which now man NATO's primary defense lines; (3) initial or "rapid" augmentation forces, consisting of American and British dual-based units, French forces (at least on a contingency basis), German territorials, and Dutch ready reserve units; and (4) longer-term augmentation forces—both from European reserves and from the so-called strategic reserve forces of the United States— composed of active and reserve personnel.

The present NATO posture understandably concentrates on the second of these elements—the active M-day forces located in Central Europe. But if the goal is a posture that will be politically sustainable throughout the 1970s in a climate of low threat perception (and high interest in détente), then it might be possible to maintain an equally credible deterrent force—with a good capability for coping with the smaller (and less unlikely) contingencies—by a somewhat different distribution of these elements.

For example, instead of being deployed for linear defense as they are at present, the main maneuver forces could be organized into task forces for defense in depth, so that they could counterattack any penetration of the forward defense. These maneuvering units might consist of a smaller number of higher quality armored and mechanized divisions—say, two German corps of three divisions each, one Benelux corps, one British corps (including a Canadian contribution), and one American corps—which could serve as the Supreme Allied Commander's theater reserve and be employed wherever the need was most critical. One of the three American divisions making up this corps might become air mobile, once that capability was no longer needed in Vietnam.

This restructuring of the main maneuver forces would free some resources to improve the specialized forward-defense units. These could be designed specifically for that role and armed with antitank weapons, but not with heavy (and expensive) armor and mobility. Roughly 100 battalion-sized groups of about 1,000 men each, mostly from the Bundeswehr, might man such a forward defense network, with some nuclear support detachments and with substantial allied liaison elements, including American and other armored cavalry forces as the link to the main maneuver forces.

The defense potential of this network could be supplemented by defended barriers and pre-emplaced demolitions where terrain permitted. And the active-duty groups could be strengthened by an organized militia drawn from the specific local area involved. (A similar idea was advanced by Colonel von Bonin in the early debates over German rearmament and has been restudied with growing interest by the present West German Defense Ministry.[41]) The antitank potential of such modern "minutemen" could be highly significant, provided they were properly trained and equipped.

This posture would assure that any aggression would meet an immediate response without either emphasizing or eliminating tactical nuclear options.

Against the contingency of a massive buildup on the other side, better organization and additional resources could also be put into the third element of reserves, with a view to making them more "ready" as well as building them into longer-term augmentation forces. In such a revised NATO force structure, the United States might be expected to maintain an "army" consisting of one high-quality active-duty corps and one "cadre" corps designed to maintain prepositioned equipment for men to be flown from the United States in the event of crisis. Thus three divisions would be deployed in the United States, plus the cadre and their supporting units in Europe; this would mean that a division slice of 30,000 to 40,000 men could be withdrawn from the present U.S. forces in Europe. Under this concept, the forces withdrawn would have to be maintained at full readiness in the United States, unless one of the strategic reserve divisions were to be shifted from an active to a reserve status. On the other hand, the allies, especially the Germans, could pay a much larger share of the logistic and maintenance costs for the cadre corps, thus easing the balance-of-payments cost to the United States.

Restructuring along these lines could offer at least small savings for all NATO countries in the central region, as well as for the United States. The Dutch could make good use of their effective ready reserves; the Germans could use their trained manpower pool more effectively—without political repercussions; and opportunities would arise for improving the quality and readiness of British and Belgian ground forces without increasing costs. On the other hand, this posture would probably furnish a smaller potential for sustained combat than that afforded by the present NATO forces. Thus it might not meet the Germans' political need for a maximum emphasis on forward defense. Still, the four elements should be adequate to maintain an effective deterrent in present and likely future circumstances, and to provide insurance against a renewed crisis atmosphere. Perhaps most important of all, this concept might offer a chance to stabilize the NATO posture on a politically and economically sustainable basis throughout the 1970s (again, if reductions become necessary).

In an ideal world, this restructuring could be carried out at acceptable military cost. In the real world, it would carry severe disadvantages. Western Europeans and Russians alike might well view any such scheme as the start of American disengagement. The effect could be a significant degradation of NATO's ability both to deter the East and to reassure the West.

So the best answer, if unilateral cuts in U.S. forces must eventually be made, might be to make any naval adjustments that prove feasible and then move toward a balanced—though not necessarily equal—reduction across the board. Given the undesirability of reducing combat forces, these reductions might have to be concentrated in the administrative and support area. Since the potential reduction in this area is at best fairly small, one might assemble a package of across-the-board cuts of up to 5 percent or possibly (by reducing manning levels) a maximum of 10 percent, which would concentrate on the support and back-up area for all three services and affect initial combat potential only marginally. This seems consistent with the judgment suggested at the start of this section: that cuts of 5–10 percent would be tolerable.

A decision to make more substantial reductions of ground forces would almost certainly dictate a restructuring of NATO's entire position on the central front, possibly along the lines outlined above and with the uncertain effects indicated. The political-military balance in Central Europe is precarious at best. The less it is adjusted, the less the risk of its being upset—unless the adjustment results either from mutual East-West troop reductions or from increased Western European defense efforts or cooperation.

4

Why Europe Doesn't Do More

EUROPEAN reactions to partial withdrawals of U.S. forces based in West Germany and elsewhere on the Continent cannot be precisely calculated. As was noted in Chapter 1, some elements in Washington believe or hope that such a reduction would inspire a substantially larger and improved European contribution to joint defense. Although this view may eventually be borne out, prospects for stronger performance by America's NATO allies must be examined in the light of several reasonably self-evident political givens.

First, Western Europe's reactions would depend on the scope of the withdrawals, their timing, the way in which they were made, the degree of consultation, and finally the judgment of various governments as to what extent the withdrawals might undermine NATO strategy and degrade security.

Second, the reaction of these governments would be more particularistic than uniform. One or two of them might conceivably feel pushed—at least initially—to increase defense efforts in one form or another; the others would either maintain current programs—again, at least initially—or begin to reduce defense commitments.

Third, and more to the point, since without exception they believe that their security is dependent on American commitments, backed by the presence of substantial U.S. forces on the Continent, an appreciable reduction in U.S. forces would arouse fears of American disengagement and collateral doubts about the feasibility of NATO security arrangements. Thus the likelihood, if not the certainty, is that American troop withdrawals—at least in present circumstances—would lead not to an increase in Western Europe's defense effort, but rather to a net decrease.

Critics of U.S. NATO commitments react to this kind of estimate by posing a valid question of continuing relevance: Why is it assumed that Europeans would not react to a reduced American presence by making a larger collective commitment to their own defense? The question can best be answered, first, by looking at the external political environment and the distribution of power; second, by examining the constraints on political action within Western Europe.

The External Political Environment

The East-West environment has been treated in detail in Chapter 2, but it may be useful here to elaborate its implications for Western European attitudes toward the United States, while also looking more generally at transatlantic relations.

Western Europe exists not as a bloc capable of unitary action but as an assortment of small and middle-sized states that in no way offer a viable alternative to the American role in balancing Soviet power. Indeed, implicit in European anxieties about the reliability of American guarantees is a belief that neither time nor circumstance has altered the bipolar character of the European security system. Hence, Europeans would interpret any but very modest American troop withdrawals as meaning that European security was becoming less important—no longer "vital"—to the United States, or as meaning that Washington's assessment of the Soviet threat to Western Europe's security and political integrity had been scaled down.

The irony is that the progress, however uneven, of Western Europeans toward greater economic cohesion and political identity of view does not allow them to figure more prominently in the management of their own defense. Their dependence on a credible American military commitment—and presence—is no less than it ever was, their incentive to provide a European alternative no greater. The tenacity of current security arrangements, although a direct consequence of the distribution of power, is reinforced by related trends.

First, the strategic arms limitation talks (SALT) between the two great powers concern Western Europe's security at least as much as America's, yet Western Europe is not represented and can influence the dialogue only to the extent that consultation with Washington affects the American position. The relative weakness of Western Europe's position is even more apparent when it is recalled that London, Paris, and occasionally Bonn were represented in most of the direct negotiations with Moscow during the 1950s and early 1960s. Except for the Berlin issue, and despite signs of growing support for a European security conference, the trend is away from joint Atlantic contact with Moscow in favor of the Washington-Moscow dialogue long feared by numerous Europeans.

These bilateral arms control negotiations have somewhat blurred the normally clear identity of political interest between the United States and its NATO partners vis-à-vis the Soviet Union. The Treaty on the Non-Proliferation of Nuclear Arms (NPT) encouraged the impression of thaw in the political climate and of improved prospects for negotiation. It appeared to carry the broad purpose of checking the spread of nuclear weapons another step beyond the 1963 Partial Nuclear Test Ban Treaty. But Western Europeans, by and large, did not share Washington's satisfaction with what to them seems a self-denying ordinance that merely forbids the great powers to do something—abetting nuclear proliferation—they would not do in any case. Moreover, following the collapse of the proposed multilateral force (MLF) in the winter of 1964–65, official Washington set in motion a shift in emphasis from NATO political concerns to East-West issues, notably the NPT. Although the MLF was scarcely more popular in Europe than on Capitol Hill, the shift in emphasis, especially the high priority accorded to the NPT, aroused anxiety and resentment in some Western European countries; it seemed to set them against the United States and the cause of arms limitation, while ranging Washington and Moscow on the same side of this laudable enterprise. There arose an apparent conflict of interests, or at least of viewpoints.

SALT sharpens the appearance of a growing identity of great-power interest at the arms control level, while possibly foreshadowing less harmony of view among the European NATO countries. To date, it has been relatively easy for European NATO governments to approve American positions on SALT, partly because they have had some voice in their formation. The Nixon administration not only has expressed a strong willingness to consult closely with its European allies but has in fact done so—something of a departure from past Washington performance. However, experience suggests that continued success of the consultation on SALT will depend on how Europeans react when the pressures of shifting priorities and fortuitous circumstances place a great deal more strain on the process than it has yet experienced. For example, would the administration continue to uphold allied opposition to reducing the nuclear weapons deployed on land and sea in the European theater if, as might be the case, Moscow continued to view these weapons as a component of America's strategic forces?

Another delicate issue might arise if Moscow seriously objected to continued American assistance to Great Britain's nuclear-capable weapons program, especially if Britain succeeded in "joining" Europe and then took the lead, as discussed below, in rationalizing and improving regional defense through joint European projects.

In these and other ways, pressures in Washington to reach an agreement with Moscow limiting strategic arms could disrupt the pattern of consultation within NATO. In any case, the Europeans, who now find it difficult to see where their interests lie with regard to SALT, could make the consultative process a great deal more difficult after their views have crystallized.

Indeed, the very willingness of the great powers to undertake SALT seems to formalize the principle of parity—the recognition by each party of the other's so-called assured destruction capability. Acceptance of parity may in turn be interpreted by Europeans as devaluing guarantees that date back to a period of American nuclear supremacy, just as a continuing great-power dialogue on strategic arms could be seen as foreshadowing a de facto condominium—the start of a process that would end with settlement of European affairs by the great powers without reference to European governments. Hence the European interpretation of what the great powers are doing could obscure the purposes and merits of what is actually done, whether with regard to SALT or to decisions linking NATO strategy and revised force levels. In all these ways, the growing bilateral U.S.-Soviet dialogue tends to create a feeling of helplessness in Western European countries that reinforces their belief that security policy is essentially a superpower monopoly.

A second source of Europe's reluctance to upgrade collective defense is the lessening of tensions and opening of negotiations on a number of sensitive issues that tend to make a Soviet threat even less plausible. In turn, Western Europe's incentive to maintain, let alone increase, existing levels of defense expenditures is to a considerable extent the product of American exhortation and of concern that any reduction in their defense efforts would goad the Americans into withdrawing a substantial portion of their forces.

Third, the cost and technical complexity of advanced weapons systems is on a sharply rising curve. Only Britain and France in Western Europe could lay claim to self-sufficiency—and even here the pressures of cost and of finding exterior markets for military products are likely to mean before long that joint development and procurement of advanced systems (nonnuclear) will be more a matter of necessity than of political expediency, as has been the case. As for strategic forces, a fully modern, independent, second-strike nuclear capability is beyond the reach of Britain and France operating alone or probably jointly—and the political obstacles to an all-European deterrent will remain formidable until much greater progress has been made toward political unity. Yet a serious decline of confidence in the U.S. commitment could prematurely force to the surface this issue of nuclear self-defense. Rejecting, as they probably would, the option of training and deploying more of their own soldiers, Europeans would probably react by expanding nuclear capabilities—a step for which they are far from ready politically and technically, and one that they could take only at considerable cost to conventional defense strength. Moreover, if Britain and France link their nationally controlled nuclear forces by various means, as well as expand them, they could invite pressure from partner states, especially Germany, for some kind of participatory role. Movement in this direction would arouse concerns that would complicate Europe's relations with the United States on a whole range of unrelated issues—including even trade and monetary policy—while stimulating a strong Soviet reaction as well. In short, until Western Europe is more united, any steps leading toward greater and more independent nuclear defense capabilities would probably create more problems than they would solve. In perceiving this to be the case, Europeans are left even more sharply aware of their dependence on the so-called nuclear umbrella of the United States and of the need for strong American conventional forces to make this nuclear option credible.

These and other considerations suggest that what Western European states do in the years ahead is likely to be as much or more a reaction to what the great powers do than a product of their own unrelated and independent initiatives. Decisions on U.S. NATO commitments will be critical—probably more critical than anything else. Although each of the European NATO members, France included, opposes unilateral American withdrawals, the most articulate and open aversion to the idea is found in Bonn. Defense Minister Helmut Schmidt is known to believe that such a step would lead to reduced defense spending by his government. He publicly has ruled out greater German efforts to make up the difference, stating that "lack of money, manpower and popular support would preclude such a solution—quite apart from the grave political effects it would have in the East as well as in the West."[1]

Both Schmidt and Chancellor Willy Brandt have warned that unilateral reductions could damage America's world position by catalyzing a shift in the balance of power in favor of the Soviet Union. Brandt has said, for example, that it is "not only a military problem . . . [but] a political and psychological problem as well. In at least parts of Europe, a major withdrawal of American troops . . . would be regarded as a step toward well, more or less, Soviet hegemony, as far as Europe is concerned."[2] This point of view is supported with greater or lesser degrees of intensity in diplomatic and dominant political circles throughout Western Europe.

Put differently, it is arguable, if not axiomatic, that American guarantees and military presence have a one-to-one relationship with Western Europe's sense of its own political integrity. The recurring difficulty is to maintain Europe's confidence in the bona fides of a foreign protector 3,000 miles distant, without allowing inevitable divergences and misunderstandings to obscure or even undermine the vital interests shared by Americans and Europeans.

Western Europe's view of its security is clearly influenced by a changing—or, as some would argue, transitional—political environment. As was noted above, the great-power dialogue *does* affect assumptions of Europeans about their security. Bonn's Ostpolitik will have a deep, if as yet incalculable, effect on German internal politics and perhaps on the Federal Republic's relationships East to West. The interim agreement on Berlin in turn will affect the course of Ostpolitik as well as improving the prospects for a European security conference, a Soviet proposal of impressive vintage that has acquired an aura of respectability and has blurred the effects of hard-line Soviet tactics, including the suppression of Czechoslovakia's bid for a more permissive, if no less socialist, system.

The sense of change also finds expression in the concern aroused in Western European political circles by the debate in Washington on U.S. NATO commitments and by the blend of ambiguity and indifference that seems to them, rightly or wrongly, to characterize current American attitudes toward Europe. Never mind that declining European interest in problems elsewhere in the world gradually dilutes the intimacy of relations with the United States, a global power; that the European Community has shown few signs of vindicating the hopes for political unity on which American support for the movement was based; that the passage of time is bound to affect a set of transatlantic relationships shaped in large part by the cold war.

Collateral European doubts about America's ability to cope effectively with its internal problems are fed by the somewhat contradictory but deeper concern that, in groping for a better balance between domestic priorities and international burdens, America will forget that the defense of its own interests begins in Western Europe. Europeans believe, not unreasonably, that in redressing their continent's military imbalance, the United States buys a great deal of security for itself, while maintaining a strong influence over what transpires in Western and Central Europe. U.S. forces sustain an Atlantic system that enables Americans to join with Europeans in working out not only joint Atlantic security affairs, but also an array of financial, commercial, and interconnected political matters. The United States, as well as Europe, has an enormous stake in this system, within which American power and resources are thought to dominate the economic as well as the security area. American investment in Western Europe continues to grow rapidly, exceeding $20 billion. American-controlled multinational companies have altered traditional ownership patterns, and they strongly influence currency movements. This other American role sharpens the Europeans' sense of dependence and causes them to wonder why so many Americans fail to perceive that the European-based U.S. forces are essential not only to Western security, but also to the stability of the Atlantic system from which the United States benefits so greatly. It is one more reason why a European perception, whether valid or not, of a diminishing American role would be more likely to stimulate a sense of futility than compensatory self-defense efforts.

Constraints on European Political Action

The logic of European security suggests that current NATO arrangements should not be seriously affected by the changing external political environment described above. In fact, considerations like those adduced by the critics quoted in Chapter 1 may dictate efforts to rebalance the present NATO system. Modest steps in this direction are under way. It may be that only further moves in this direction—finding some means of rebalancing NATO and of introducing a new political dynamic—will make it be possible to prevent a slow deterioration of this structure.

The priority need is thus not only to discourage Europeans from running down their security forces, but also to rebalance NATO by increasing their defense efforts—although prospects are doubtful that European NATO governments will choose to do more than hold the line on current defense budgets. Defense costs are rising in Europe, just as they are in the United States. Western Europe's concern with public welfare and education—the latter normally a source of higher expenditure than defense—is rising there just as here. The military vocation is even less popular in Western Europe than in America; aversion to military service is found in all Western European countries, not least in the chief regional powers—Britain, France, and West Germany. It is a question both of recruitment and of developing cadres of trained officers and noncommissioned ranks. The problem could dictate a trend away from complex, high-performance weapons systems toward simpler weapons consistent with shorter tours of duty; but it also reinforces sentiment to reduce, or at least not to increase, existing defense forces.

Probably, then, NATO will not be rebalanced by increased European effort in the period directly ahead; merely maintaining some approximation of the status quo may be difficult enough. Any new political dynamic that would lead to effective joint Western European defense will be, at best, a long time in coming. It will develop only if and when Western Europe manages significant progress toward political unity. Current tendencies suggest that movement toward closer political cooperation and organization will be slow; that, barring upheavals or reversals of existing defense arrangements, the attention of Western European governments over the next five to seven years will be largely absorbed in reaching agreement on joint arrangements for problems not directly related to security—notably money and payments, agriculture, commercial policy, tax harmonization, and industrial organization. Conventional European thinking holds that some combination of economic cooperation and integration must precede steps toward any advanced degree of political unity, whatever the model. And defense, it is universally held, will not be a stalking-horse for political unity. Joint defense arrangements among European NATO countries are regarded as among the last of a long series of steps in the unifying process.

Such thinking conforms to the realities and perhaps even the logic of the current situation. And if it arouses little hope for a united Europe moving gradually from under the American wing, neither does it exclude steps in that direction. It is a frankly pragmatic attitude; as such, it discourages some Europeans who fear that, in the absence of bold initiatives, the impulse to unify will be lost.

Another and more controlling view is that Europe has been buffeted in recent years by an excess of exhortation and visionary thinking, whether articulated by the Monnet integrationists or by General de Gaulle in his quest for a French-led coalition of states. What is required, according to this view, is less inspiration and more steady, undramatic attention to problems that fall within the competence of the European Community. This suggests moving toward a working model for the European Community that would enable joint institutions to deal more effectively with the bureaucracies of member countries without usurping bureaucratic authority or indeed raising the issue of derogation of sovereignty. Achieving this better division of labor between governments and joint institutions, reaching agreement on issues affecting the Brussels negotiations with Great Britain, and dealing at the same time with the essentially economic questions at hand—all this, it is argued, must take precedence over other matters of concern to Western Europe. However realistic, this attitude risks bearing out its critics. The European movement has been animated more by a political idea than by fixed economic goals; to ignore this fact is to risk undermining functional progress toward integrating the economies of member countries and their political purpose as well.

Much of the enthusiasm for the enterprise has vanished. Time and a laggard performance in fulfilling certain goals of the Rome Treaty would account for this in part. But the disenchantment is also partly traceable to the steady decline of the political incentive to "build Europe." This incentive was founded on both hope and a perceived need to replace the traditional order with joint arrangements—even institutions—for managing problems no longer manageable at the level of European states. Critics have retrospectively labeled this kind of thinking as "romantic," as evoking a model built on "myths," yet the essence of the European movement probably lies in its ideal—its possibly romantic impulse to avoid the mistakes of the past by creating a structure or system capable of containing and reconciling the diverse interests of its members. This is not to suggest that public opinion in any major European country would ever have explicitly favored a derogation of sovereignty. The issue is not as simple as that. It is rather that the European Community's great strength was the spirit that enabled member states for a time to yield on points of national interest in favor of a larger Community interest.

Although that time appears to have passed, it would be misleading —certainly premature—to write off the possibility that Western Europe will one day achieve a substantial degree of political unity. The vision of an integrated European Community is still supported, or considered possible, not as an idea firing the popular imagination but as a means of problem-solving on a broad scale. Perhaps more importantly, European unity is regarded less as a panacea than as an alternative to and a check on other tendencies, especially the nationalism that has regathered strength throughout Europe. The point is that nationalism in its present form is not necessarily pernicious but that it sets limits on Western Europe's progress and its independence from the superpowers.

It would be equally misleading to suggest that the idea of European unity is again in fashion, or that events of the past three years—principally the departure of General de Gaulle, the Soviet invasion of Czechoslovakia, and the Community enlargement negotiations—have significantly revived the tendency toward integration. Nothing so broad is happening or is likely to happen in the near future. What may be said is that the Common Market will continue; this was by no means a certainty two years ago. Moreover, it is now likely that Great Britain will take part as a full member, although this too seemed doubtful three years ago. Broad agreement exists among the Six, as well as among Great Britain and the other candidates for membership, on the desirability of moving toward a monetary union during the 1970s. And while sharp disagreement persists on the modalities of joint monetary arrangements, declaratory adherence to the goal may well imply eventual acceptance of substantial economic integration with a fair-sized dose of supranationalism.

London, Paris, Bonn

The negotiations in Brussels and the events that led up to them have brought to the surface some basic questions concerning the future of the European Community. Member governments and Great Britain are being forced to ponder the possibilities and limitations of the existing structure and to adjust their sights accordingly. The result—what the Western Europeans actually do about defense, for example—will depend largely on two closely related considerations: (1) the course of the relationship between the two great powers and their actions on issues affecting Europe, and (2) the degree to which the key Western European capitals—London, Bonn, and Paris—can narrow their differences and develop a progressively broader identity of political views on issues as they develop.

The British Position

Britain's position is curiously paradoxical. More than any other European capital, London accepts the need for Europeans to assume a greater portion of the responsibility for European security in the years directly ahead. Britain's defense posture has been largely shorn of its East-of-Suez attributes and reoriented toward continental Europe. Whitehall has made modest proposals to establish a European "identity" within NATO, and both the Ministry of Defense and the Foreign Office are increasingly preoccupied with making European defense more "cost-effective."

London's continental partners have reacted with varying degrees of skepticism, fearing that purely European initiatives will furnish Washington with a pretext for withdrawing troops from Germany. Yet Britain's perception of the need for deep American involvement in Europe's affairs—whether economic or political-military—is instinctive and traditional, more so than that of the continentals, whose attitudes on this point are complex and mercurial. While often annoyed at the long American shadow, the continental Europeans are generally more aroused than Britain by any development that might encourage a decline in America's European involvement. Thus they have tended to resist Britain's Europe-oriented defense initiatives, while insisting in another context that in establishing its European bona fides, Britain must make a clear commitment to the supranational objectives of the Rome Treaty—and never mind that France and West Germany show little if any affinity for such goals. Indeed, London harbors the only major bureaucracy in Europe that might now support a European defense organization with modest supranational attributes. Even Britain's declared willingness to go just as far as the other countries toward integration can be accepted as genuine, if only because it commits Her Majesty's government to relatively little. The British perceive that, for the moment, supranationalism commands largely rhetorical support on the Continent. De Gaulle's opposition to integrationist objectives enabled many other European politicians to continue masquerading as members of the Community faith while silently grateful for the brakes he applied.

The French Position

Although the Pompidou government has had a moderating effect, official French attitudes and policy are not likely to undergo sweeping change—certainly not in the near future. Even before de Gaulle left, however, French cooperation with NATO was becoming closer, and

French policy was edging away from its rhetorical neutrality of 1966–68.

In time, France might seek a link with, if not membership in, NATO's Nuclear Planning Group (NPG), a notably useful instrument comprising Britain, West Germany, Italy, and the United States as permanent members and three smaller countries as rotating members on an eighteen-month cycle. The NPG was created on U.S. initiative about five years ago; its utility depends largely on Washington's willingness to disclose hitherto tightly held information regarding defense planning and nuclear strategy. Nuclear planning requires not only that political direction be assured before, during, and after the outbreak of hostilities, at whatever level, but also that European governments understand why, how, and with what effect nuclear weapons might be used. Not until the NPG was formed did the war plans of the Supreme Allied Commander, Europe (SACEUR) become available to NATO defense ministers in Europe.

A major part of the NPG's work is related to tactical nuclear weapons deployed in Europe. For France to remain apart from this activity is unnatural, not only because of the French political and geographical position but also because of its developing tactical nuclear capability. Probably the United States and Britain would welcome France to the NPG, while the continentals, by and large, would be less willing to share their privileged role with a country whose NATO participation remains highly selective and that is not a member of NATO'S fourteen-nation Defense Planning Committee (DPC). Moreover, French participation would pose real problems: Since much of the NPG's guidance comes from the DPC, France, as an NPG member, might find itself implementing decisions taken without French participation. And even if France someday wanted to take part in the DPC—a doubtful assumption—it is unlikely that other members would allow France to participate without recommitting forces to NATO.

In time, France's attitude toward joint European defense—as distinct from NATO—may become more positive. European cooperation does not inject the issue of American domination, and France may find that it can carry forward major defense-related projects only by placing some of them in a European setting. To date, most of Europe's joint projects have arisen from ad hoc political arrangements, with France close to the center owing to a strong bargaining position vis-à-vis Britain and Germany. But this pattern is changing. Some European projects have entered advanced planning and even prototype stages without French participation.

France, in short, may find itself in the unfamiliar role of *demandeur* more often now than in the past. France has a narrower industrial base than Britain. In some defense-related industries, however, France has achieved a high degree of excellence, especially in research and development. France designs and builds combat aircraft, for example, with a smaller capital investment and in less time than American competitors. Nonetheless, the problem of maintaining a competitive edge and having larger and more assured access to the European aerospace market may eventually dictate French support for a European defense procurement organization. Progress in this direction would clearly require joint European decisions on strategy and force planning.

This situation suggests a process that will emerge, if at all, over a long period of time. It is most unlikely that in the first half of the 1970s European NATO governments will achieve a degree of defense cooperation that would enable them to compensate for a major U.S. force reduction. France's attitude on regional defense cooperation is less negative than the utterances of French leaders might indicate, just as Britain's attitude may prove to be less aggressive than it appears. Both countries may eventually want to move forward, but even then progress is likely to be uneven and slow. Finally, much will depend on how German thinking evolves.

The West German Position

Of these three national positions, Bonn's is the most ambiguous, chiefly because as always the Federal Republic is tugged in different directions, and because its great economic power has not yet significantly extended German political margins. The Brandt government has scattered the public record with statements that its Eastern policy (Ostpolitik) must be sustained and reinforced by a Western policy devoted to maintaining collective security arrangements and to expanding and strengthening the Common Market. For Bonn, it is axiomatic that the Eastern policy relies directly on American guarantees and a continued strong American military presence in Germany. Without this presence, Bonn would be negotiating with the Warsaw Pact countries from a position of relative weakness.

That is the argument, and it is persuasive. Yet viewed from a somewhat different angle, it means that the United States is directly involved in German contacts with the Soviet Union, whether it approves or disapproves of what they produce. The four-power accord on Berlin was the result of German initiative and pressure, the idea being that progress on Berlin would legitimatize submission of the nonaggression treaty between the Federal Republic and the USSR to the Bundestag for ratification.

Although Bonn's chief allies—the United States, Britain, and France —support Brandt's Ostpolitik, they are highly sensitive to such potential hazards as the effect on German policy and politics of exaggerated German expectations or failure. They recognize that Bonn's concessions on German frontiers and its acceptance of the principle of two German states "within a single nation" were inevitable and even desirable. But they believe that Bonn has few concessions left to make that would not compromise its links with the West or alter the status quo in ways better suited to Moscow's purposes than to those of Washington, London, and Paris. The Berlin accord, however, has offered some encouragement regarding Moscow's readiness for compromise. One effect of Brandt's Ostpolitik has been to outflank East Germany—to expose the Pankow regime to potential isolation whenever other Eastern European states begin to normalize their relations with Bonn. In turn, the uncompromising figure of Walter Ulbricht, the last communist of the Lenin-Stalin era, has been superseded by Erich Honecker and a regime more amenable to the vagaries of Soviet policy.

To date, however, the main effect of Ostpolitik has been to confirm Bonn's acceptance of two German states, of existing German
borders, and of the absence of any prospect for reunification in the
near future. Chancellor Brandt's government, notwithstanding its resolve to avoid weakening its Western links and policies, has a vested
interest in earning dividends on its Ostpolitik. As the process of moderating German relations to the East continues, Bonn's interest in the
progress of Ostpolitik may become still more compelling and the
prospect of failure increasingly intolerable. This is not to underrate
the Brandt government's perception of the hazards implicit in an active Ostpolitik but rather to suggest that the policy does carry risk—
that unless Ostpolitik remains solidly linked with a durable Western
policy, its failure would leave the Federal Republic isolated and
vulnerable to intimidation.

As for Western European policy, the signs are that the Brandt government is no more attracted than was its immediate predecessors to
the kind of tightly integrated European Community structure that
could limit the Federal Republic's maneuverability vis-à-vis Eastern
Europe. Bonn has actively supported British entry into an enlarged
Community in which Norway, Denmark, and Ireland would participate as full members. Probably Bonn will also support associate mem-
berships for neutral states like Sweden and Austria. Inside the Community, Brandt will probably encourage integrationist tendencies
regarding tax and monetary issues. He probably will assure that East
Germany becomes, in time, a full trading partner of the Community,
since the Rome Treaty provides that no trade barriers exist between
the two German states. Finally, Brandt will doubtless also try to
maintain the close bilateral military cooperation with Britain inau-
gurated by Chancellor Kiesinger and Prime Minister Wilson, and
perhaps will try to stimulate progressively closer links with Pompidou's France.

Less certain is solid West German support for multilateral defense
cooperation at the European level. Soviet hostility to intra-Western
European defense cooperation might—or might not—discourage any
incentive that Bonn would otherwise have to reexamine its position on

the issue. German views during negotiations on the NPT are worth recalling; Bonn pressed hard for interpretations that would not forbid the deployment of nuclear weapons by a united Western European Community. In brief, any estimate of how a German government would respond at some unspecified date to a European defense initiative must remain highly speculative. The U.S. attitude may well be the controlling factor; the Germans will want solid assurances that intra-European defense cooperation could not lead to a lessening of U.S. involvement.

Germany's neighbors and allies perceive that time and events have maneuvered the Federal Republic's latent political power closer to the surface. It can be reasonably argued that such power is not an exploitable asset, precisely because Germany lies at the center of the power balance, dependent on the Seventh Army for security and on Moscow for good relations with the East. Actually, the mere fact of West German power—economic and political—is important, whatever the constraints on its use. It is a factor that neighboring and basically weaker societies to the East and West must take into account. Although such power reduces German incentives to make a strong commitment in any direction, it is an element in the calculations of every government involved in European security.

Inevitably, the creation of a closely organized European political and defense structure will depend as much on German preferences and strength of purpose as on any other consideration. Time and a changing political context are gradually moving France and Britain away from traditional preferences and attitudes. For these two old societies, each burdened with the frustrations and failures of the recent past as well as with a sense of declining power, acceptable alternatives to European organization are losing plausibility. But West Germany confronts what could be sharply conflicting interests. And it is important to remember that just as the Seventh Army provides the stability on which Bonn's Ostpolitik relies, America's NATO commitments stabilize the political environment in which Germany and other Western European countries feel free to integrate their efforts in some areas while rationalizing methods of cooperation in others.

Western Europe's Defense Options

Although a broad range of defense options can be conceived for Western Europe, the term "options" may be extravagant, since European NATO governments would be limited by public opinion and the other constraints already noted in any effort to develop a substantially greater defense capability. For example, it most unlikely that, whatever the scope of future regional efforts, Western Europe would seek, much less achieve, superpower status. Although the full panoply of nuclear weapons and support systems used by the great powers to practice deterrence is theoretically within the grasp of a united Europe, it is probably not a feasible objective in political terms. Assuming the contrary will be the case, it is even more unlikely that Western Europe would at the same time create conventional defense forces on a scale adequate to permit playing the great-power game or sufficient to compensate for the withdrawal of the American units.

These would seem to be the broad possibilities:

1. Maintaining the status quo, with each European NATO government (France included) seeking to maintain or even tighten its defense links with the United States, while rejecting proposals designed to promote significantly closer European political-military cooperation.

2. Maintaining the status quo, with emphasis on bilateral intra-Western European arrangements in the area of defense and defense-related technology. Some of these arrangements might involve more than two countries, perhaps even most of the principal states of Western Europe, but on an ad hoc basis.

3. Moving in stages toward a European defense authority endowed with considerable central decision-making power.

4. Reducing European defense efforts, primarily in response to a reduction of the American military presence.

It bears repeating that a trend toward any one of these four illustrative possibilities would depend on actions of the superpowers and on the East-West political environment at least as much as it would on the evolution of the European unity movement.

The first possibility—confirming the status quo while emphasizing close links with Washington—would give the United States continuing flexibility in its dealings both with major Western European countries and with Moscow. Furthermore, it would run little risk of discouraging European NATO governments from procuring a large portion of their advanced weapon systems and components at lower cost from the American shelf. Such a trend, if dominant, would also postpone the day when Western Europe could begin to take on a larger share of the NATO military burden.

The second possibility—a continuation of the status quo, combined with a push toward intra-European bilateral arrangements—could mean a shifting network of relationships that might find its strongest expression in a revival of some near equivalent of the Anglo-French entente cordiale. It could eventually mean an entente nucléaire, with Great Britain and France jointly targeting their still nationally controlled nuclear forces and possibly exchanging data and experience regarding the technology of nuclear-capable systems. Here the benefits in purely technological terms would be weighted on France's side, given Britain's longer experience, broader weapons base, and, of course, the special relationship with the United States. But in the long run, French experience in solid-fuel ballistic missile technology, production techniques, and program management might usefully complement Britain's warhead and guidance technology. There are, as well, the intangibles of French enthusiasm and French determination not to be swept aside.

Growing interest in the possibility of Anglo-French nuclear cooperation raises a number of questions, however. The first is its feasibility in terms of the current attitudes and priorities of the two governments, which in turn would depend in part on French willingness (still unlikely) to move back toward significantly closer cooperation with NATO—presumably to integrate French nuclear weapons in the NATO targeting system. Second, the American view of Anglo-French nuclear cooperation has not crystallized, but more explicit assurances concerning French political and strategic attitudes toward NATO defense are likely to be required before the United States would release Britain from the constraints of the bilateral agreements governing the special U.S.-U.K. nuclear arrangements. In assessing the U.S. attitude, the question of SALT and other great-power negotiations might also arise. Should the entente nucléaire show signs of becoming a germinal European military organization, with coparticipation by West Germany at the nuclear level, strong objections from Moscow could be expected.

Nor can Bonn's attitude toward Anglo-French nuclear collaboration be precisely calculated. If such arrangements served primarily to tighten French links with NATO, Bonn might well approve. If, on the other hand, the entente nucléaire seemed designed to create a strictly bilateral alternative to reliance on NATO arrangements, Bonn (along with other Western European capitals) would doubtless object strongly. An arrangement whereby Anglo-French nuclear cooperation would be fortified by a West German financial contribution, in return for which Bonn acquired a participatory role in the planning and targeting of nuclear weapons, might have strong appeal. It might be regarded—at least in Bonn—as a precursor to a European strategic option opening new doors to Germany rather than as a device for better enabling Britain and France to continue deploying nuclear weapons.

All that may be confidently said at the moment is that Britain is unlikely to move toward any kind of entente nucléaire in the absence of NATO-related French political concessions that Paris is not now prepared to make. Britain's special nuclear arrangements with the United States will have a higher priority so long as they are in force and so long as American NATO commitments remain firm. Still, the situation could change. The special U.S.-U.K. agreements are renewable at the pleasure of the Congress, and Britain may one day want to hedge by moving toward a closer link with France in the area of advanced weapons systems. In turn, the French might view such an alignment as a means of balancing German power, as one way eventually to reduce the French investment in time and resources required to maintain credible strategic nuclear weapons, and as a means of making Britain appear more European—thus justifying France's acquiescence in an active British role in the European Community. Moreover, although the declaratory position of each government on the nuclear issue is unacceptable to the other, the French position might gradually bend, especially as the problem of fitting French forces into a rational strategic framework sharpens and the European political context continues to evolve.

The question is whether piecemeal steps of the kind that can be envisioned under this option would create a framework within which European governments could achieve a degree of joint defense effort that would safely permit a major reduction of U.S. forces.

The third possibility—a variety of defense-related measures taken within a European defense authority—is perhaps the least likely in the short or even middle term. Britain, once inside the European Community, could become the major force behind the movement toward such an authority; but Britain alone could not persuade reluctant continentals to join in. West German reservations about full-blooded European defense arrangements are reflected in an article by Defense Minister Helmut Schmidt, who compared such "high flying plans" as the European Defense Community, which "foundered on the mountains of national self-interest," with the present need for "pragmatism and gradualism."[3]

Bonn's attitude is matched by that of Paris. In time, however, it may be that broad European defense initiatives will find the terrain less treacherous, especially if it is clear that the aim is not to replace but to complement more effectively the preponderant American role, eventually effecting a mutually acceptable reduction.

The fourth possibility would be an overall reduction in Western European defense programs by governments that had concluded, rightly or wrongly, that the collective security system was no longer viable. From every point of view, this is obviously the least desirable answer. Whether it is chosen will depend more directly on American decisions than on European preferences.

Still, in the long run, the Europeans themselves must decide whether to find some corrective to the anomaly of dependence on the United States for their security. At present, it appears that through inertia and the absence of acceptable alternatives, the status quo will endure.

For how long? At what point will this reliance on an external power be mocked by events and unforeseeable developments? When, if ever, will the Europeans begin to hedge against an uncertain future by coming back to a "European" solution for the dilemma of Western European defense? At present, the trend toward bilateral arrangements is significantly stronger than the "European" impulse. In the short run, the three major European capitals are likely to tackle defense matters —especially procurement—in an ad hoc manner; but the tensions, competitive pressures, and wasteful duplication inherent in these ad hoc arrangements may eventually lead them to the more cost-effective Community method. A greater incentive toward movement in this direction could emerge from Europe's inability to reach effective negotiating positions vis-à-vis the United States through the North Atlantic Council as it is now organized. Europeans may come to see that steady and productive transatlantic consultation may depend on how they decide to approach the Americans—whether they can speak with something approaching a single voice on NATO force planning, strategy, SALT, MBFR, and other issues.

If and as the unity movement builds up momentum at the political as well as defense levels, European governments may eventually contemplate subsuming current NATO arrangements in a new joint U.S.-Western European security alliance that would place the respective roles of the partners—the United States and a European Community—in better balance. Americans can do little to encourage such a process other than to avoid discouraging it. And however ambivalent Europeans may be about relying on American commitments and the strong American presence, the incentive to rebalance security arrangements has yet to emerge.

After more than two decades of experience, NATO has become a society whose members instinctively look to the strongest among them for direction. The European governments would rather coordinate defense arrangements with Washington than with each other;

meetings of the Eurogroup of NATO defense ministers have accomplished relatively little.

Western Europe's inertia and sense of inadequacy vis-à-vis the great powers can be easily explained in terms of the political conditions and attitudes discussed in this chapter. But finding the incentive to overcome these attitudes and to extend Western Europe's political cohesion and influence will mean overcoming obstacles that are as much psychological as political—and that are rooted in decades of frustration, instability, and dependence.

5

The Financial Cost of Alliance

COST is the predominant—sometimes the exclusive—consideration in much of the public debate about keeping U.S. troops in Europe. The issue is most frequently stated as follows: Can the United States afford to continue its NATO commitment in this form? Underlying this statement of the problem is the assumption that a reduction in forces stationed in Europe automatically will cut budgetary as well as foreign exchange costs, thus freeing resources for meeting domestic priorities and easing the balance-of-payments constraint on economic policy decisions. Both the issue and the assumption merit careful examination.

Three questions are involved:

1. What is the net resource or budget cost of the American military commitment to NATO? Widely different measures are used, depending on the meaning attached to the concept. We maintain a variety of forces for European contingencies, some located in Europe and some in the United States. Would costs be less if the numbers in Europe were reduced but total forces remained unchanged? Would it help much if European NATO countries shared the cost of operating American facilities in Europe? Would a reduction in forces stationed in Europe permit the United States to reduce total forces and hence

reduce costs? How, in other words, do the forces stationed in Europe relate to the total U.S. force structure?

2. What foreign exchange cost does this commitment entail? There are problems of measurement here as well. But the main issues concern the relationship of these foreign exchange costs to the international financial policies of European NATO countries. Would the U.S. dollar automatically be strengthened if troops were pulled back from Europe? More generally, how do foreign exchange expenditures and receipts resulting from NATO troop stationing arrangements affect the operation of the international monetary system and the position of the dollar in that system?

3. Is the United States contributing too much and Western Europe too little when judged by the relative security interests of each in NATO and by an acceptable standard for measuring the respective burdens, including some accounting of comparative economic capabilities?

This chapter examines each of these questions in turn. They are all fundamental, but they are also logically separable. Lumping them together, as is usually done, tends to obscure the range of options open to the United States, the costs applicable to each option, and possible areas of U.S.-European action that could affect U.S. choices.

U.S. Budgetary Issues

U.S. budgetary outlays for NATO are a relatively new factor in the public debate on U.S. troop levels in Europe. Estimates began appearing in published articles and congressional testimony only as recently as 1969. They have sometimes been used to show how much the United States could save by withdrawing troops from Europe, at other times to demonstrate to Europeans that an improvement in their financial contribution to common defense arrangements, at relatively small cost, would have a multiplier effect in helping the United States to maintain its far more costly commitment to the defense of Europe.

How much we spend for NATO can be calculated by adding up

the cost of U.S. forces stationed in Europe and of forces stationed in the United States that are specifically earmarked for NATO or oriented to European contingencies. Indeed, the justification for a major part of the U.S. military budget rests on this specific mission. Nevertheless, allocating the cost of U.S. military forces according to the need to meet contingencies in geographic areas requires arbitrary judgments that have a substantial quantitative effect on the results. Furthermore, the concept of NATO budgetary costs itself is not without difficulty; in one sense it overstates the actual cost of NATO to the United States; in another sense it understates this cost.

For example, this calculation of cost does not imply that the United States could, with equanimity, do entirely without these forces if NATO were abolished. Without NATO, the U.S. defense budget might change very little. Some, and conceivably all of these forces, or their equivalents, might still be required, but they would be positioned and structured differently and perhaps justified by different reasoning.* In this sense, budget costs for the defense of Western Europe, as usually defined, greatly overstate the *incremental* cost of U.S. military forces arising from NATO responsibilities.

Nor does the calculation mean that these particular forces are all that would be committed to Europe in the event of military action. U.S. ground and tactical air units stationed in the United States as strategic reserve forces or as forces assigned to meet contingencies in the Pacific could also be used in Europe during an emergency. (Conversely, as envisaged in current defense doctrine, some forces maintained for European contingencies could be used in Asia in an emergency.) Further, in estimating budget spending for NATO, no allowance is made for the cost of U.S. strategic forces since, with

---

* One might even argue that the abolition of NATO would result in an increase in U.S. military budgets, if as a consequence Western Europe's defense efforts were cut back and the United States believed that its security interests required additional U.S. military capability to make up for some part of the loss. Alternatively, the consequence could be a drastic downgrading of the U.S. view of its security interests in Europe and hence a reduction in the U.S. force structure and defense costs. But deactivation of *all* U.S. forces maintained for European contingencies would be inconceivable if for no other reason than that it would leave gaps in requirements for the core defense of the United States.

very limited exceptions, they are not assigned geographically. Yet a portion of these forces presumably covers Soviet intermediate-range nuclear weapons that threaten Europe, not the United States, and the strategic forces as a whole are critical to holding the alliance together and to its deterrent value. These reasons explain why the geographic concept of budget cost understates the cost of the U.S. contribution to NATO.

Problems also arise in the geographical allocation of overhead costs such as administration, research and development, intelligence and communications, central supply and maintenance, training, medical, and other general personnel activities, and retirement pay. These costs are responsive to changes in the size of forces, but in greatly varying degree. Making some allowance for them in computing the cost of NATO forces is not an exact science, but making no allowance for them at all would considerably understate the cost of these forces.

These difficulties simply underline the fact that to a large degree military forces, like money, are fungible. They can be viewed as insurance against more than one contingency in Europe, against contingencies in Asia, and also against contingencies that might arise in the Western Hemisphere or that might threaten the continental United States. Analysis of whether the United States could save money by withdrawing troops from Europe must rest, therefore, not simply on actions taken in Europe but on how such actions affect decisions relating to total U.S. forces. And these decisions, in turn, will depend on how much insurance against risks the United States is prepared to pay for and how Americans rate risks as between contingencies in Europe and contingencies elsewhere.

Possible Areas of Saving

Given these considerations, what are the various ways of measuring how much NATO costs the United States, and what conclusions do these calculations offer for saving budget money by bringing U.S. troops back from Europe or by other means? The first way is to measure only the costs of those U.S. forces actually stationed in Europe.

This is the narrowest definition, but it is the most immediately relevant to the debate on troop levels.

Stationed in Europe are more than four U.S. Army divisions (virtually all in Germany, including Berlin), seven tactical air wings (in Germany, the United Kingdom, and Turkey, plus one air wing in Spain), two attack carriers and several Polaris submarines deployed in the Mediterranean, and other naval forces assigned to NATO in the Mediterranean and Atlantic fleets.

Altogether, approximately 300,000 U.S. troops are stationed in Europe, including those afloat on NATO-assigned naval missions. The annual cost of these forces, as shown in Table 5-1, is estimated at $9.4 billion, of which $3.2 billion is for operations (personnel pay and allowances, supplies, maintenance, and transportation) and $6.2 billion

TABLE 5-1. *Estimated Annual Cost of U.S. Forces in Europe, 1970*
Millions of dollars

NATO area	Cost of operations	Investment and indirect support cost	Total cost
Central region			
Land-based forces	2,850	4,000	6,850
Naval forces afloat (Second Fleet)	150	500	650
Subtotal	3,000	4,500	7,500
Southern region			
Naval forces afloat (Sixth Fleet)	200	1,750	1,950
Subtotal	200	1,750	1,950
Total	3,200	6,250	9,450[a]

Sources: Total operating cost of U.S. forces in Europe is from testimony by Secretary of Defense Melvin R. Laird in *Military Posture*, Hearings before the House Committee on Armed Services, 92 Cong. 1 sess. (1971), Pt. 1, p. 2597. Allocation of these costs is based on the estimated distribution of U.S. forces between the central and southern regions of NATO. The cost of investment and indirect support is derived by subtracting operating costs from total costs. Total cost of forces is from Charles L. Schultze and others, *Setting National Priorities: The 1972 Budget* (Brookings Institution, 1971), pp. 54–55.

a. In testimony before the Subcommittee on International Exchanges and Payments of the Joint Economic Committee, June 21, 1971, Principal Deputy Assistant Secretary of Defense (Comptroller) Don R. Brazier estimated the cost of U.S. general purpose forces stationed in NATO Europe (including the Sixth Fleet), plus the support base required for these forces, at $7 billion to $8 billion (*Congressional Record*, daily ed., June 30, 1971, p. S10321). The difference between this estimate and the one in this table probably is accounted for by differences in the treatment of indirect support costs.

is for annual investment (military equipment and construction) and indirect support (such as administration, training, and central supply).

In terms of mission, approximately 85 percent of this cost is to support forces assigned to the defense of NATO's central region (on the German front) and 15 percent for defense of NATO's southern flank. Some of the forces are interchangeable between the two regions, but most are not. A decision to reduce total forces in Europe presumably would take into account the relative military and political risks in the two regions and would therefore fall with differing impact on the forces assigned to each. For such calculations, it is also useful to keep in mind the comparative costs of the major individual force elements: a division force costs roughly $1 billion a year; a carrier task force, about $650 million a year (almost $2 billion, with the added cost of the two carrier forces that usually back up each carrier force on station); and a tactical air wing, about $350 million a year.

A number of proposals have been advanced to reduce the burden these forces place on the U.S. budget. Some—such as economizing on low-priority military operations, greater European cost sharing, or dual basing of forces—are designed to save money, while minimizing any deterioration in the ability of these forces to carry out their present mission. These proposals are examined below. Others would require a reduction in total U.S. forces committed to NATO and therefore would explicitly diminish the U.S. contribution to the defense of Western Europe. This approach is examined later in this chapter.

CUTTING OUT FAT. A large establishment in continuous operation for over twenty years inevitably accumulates pockets of obsolescence, the U.S. military organization in Europe being no exception. Eliminating outdated military functions would not diminish combat capability. Similarly, military units or headquarters that safeguard against contingencies of very low priority represent excessively costly insurance.

Congressman Henry S. Reuss, in testimony in April 1970 before the Subcommittee on Europe of the House Committee on Foreign Affairs, suggested that each of the three services could save money by combining their headquarters in Europe. He also recommended that the Department of Defense revive the 1968–69 program known as REDCOSTE (Reduction of Costs, Europe) to streamline forces in Europe by eliminating low-priority functions. This program resulted in a reduction of 6,000 personnel and a saving of $38.3 million.[1]

Few would argue against actively pursuing such possibilities as part of a continuing process of reviewing the force structure. If they succeeded, a clear budgetary saving would be achieved, since any units eliminated would not need to be replaced in the United States. It should always be possible, as conditions change, to make technical improvements at the margin, to cut down overhead, and to keep seeking the lean look that makes for effectiveness.

Such pruning has, in fact, been under way for some time. Three major efforts to reduce duplication and eliminate marginally useful units and installations have been made in the past four years. The first, in 1966–67, was accomplished as part of the operation to relocate forces from France (FRELOC); the second, in 1968–69, was specifically aimed at cost economies in Europe and only concomitantly at force reductions (REDCOSTE); and the third, in 1970, set specific targets for expenditure reductions in fiscal 1970 (Project 703). Under the pressure of tighter defense budget appropriations, internal Defense Department reviews focused on achieving economies in European-based forces may have more bite.

Since 1966, U.S. military strength in Europe has been cut by at least 66,000, or almost one-fifth, and the number of foreign civilian employees by some 10,000.[2] Roughly half this reduction, however, resulted from the redeployment of two-thirds of a division and associated air units under the dual-basing arrangement multilaterally negotiated in 1968 and discussed in detail later in this chapter. The remainder of these force cuts were accomplished by the programs and techniques noted above—that is, by reducing or eliminating units and functions outside the divisional combat area support commands. One notable example was the elimination of Seventh Army headquarters in 1966 and the consolidation of its functions with U.S. Headquarters, Europe, resulting in a reduction of 1,276 personnel at a budget saving of $9 million a year.

Further savings of this kind seem possible through consolidating other headquarters, through speeding up the transfer of planning functions to NATO headquarters, and through greater reliance on West German forces for detailed planning of such activities as rear area security.

Essential as it is to press for such savings, it should be recognized that the potential by now must be considerably narrowed and that the amounts involved are not of a size that would appreciably affect the budgetary issue of whether the United States should keep forces in Europe and, if so, at what level.

EUROPEAN COST SHARING. Our NATO allies, either singly or in combination, could agree to pay part of the cost of supporting U.S. troops in Europe in order to ease the strain on the U.S. budget. If such payments represented an addition to the military expenditures of our allies, NATO defense capabilities would remain intact; if they were made at the expense of expenditures for European forces, total NATO defense capabilities would be diminished. How far could such a cost-sharing principle be carried? What form might it take? What would be required?

One approach might be termed a "fair share" plan. The cost of all NATO forces, whatever their national origin, could be added up and apportioned among the countries on a prearranged basis—in accordance with income, security interest, location, or some other principle. NATO infrastructure expenditures are in fact financed jointly on the basis of agreed cost shares, but they are relatively small, the current U.S. share of $50 million amounting to about one-third of the annual total. Joint financing of all NATO forces would require a complete renegotiation of the alliance and a substantial change in its implications for national control of the military forces involved. It is too late in the day for such major surgery.

Alternatively, cost sharing could be done entirely through negotiation and divorced from any particular principle. The Europeans would have to determine through periodic negotiation with the United States how much money would be necessary to keep U.S. forces in Europe at required levels and then negotiate among themselves to decide whether the cost was worth the benefits and how they would share it. Such a two-part negotiation would be a formidable process to undertake annually, or even at less frequent intervals. Moreover, the very lack of agreed principles for such a negotiation would have divisive effects and would make any resulting arrangement politically unstable. The unsatisfactory effort of the Eurogroup in NATO to negotiate a cost-sharing package in 1970, discussed below, illustrates the difficulties.

A third method, and the one usually advocated by those who propose cost sharing, is based on a commonsense approach to the problem. If the United States is willing to bear the personnel and equipment cost of its forces in Europe—the great bulk of the total cost— the Europeans should be willing to pay the cost of the local services these forces need when stationed in Europe, such as base facilities and their maintenance, housing for dependents, utilities, local taxes, and other local support activities.

Until the establishment of the Federal Republic in 1954, the Germans covered local expenditures in Germany as occupation costs. Subsequently, German payments for facilities and services provided to allied troops were negotiated under stationing cost arrangements and were greatly reduced in size. For example, German expenditures on facilities and services for U.S. troops reached a peak of some $850 million in 1952 (equivalent to about $1.5 billion in 1971 prices). By the 1960s such expenditures had become almost negligible, averaging about $25 million a year. This small figure, however, does not include the cost of police and fire protection, road maintenance, and other services provided in varying degrees to U.S. units but not recorded or budgeted as stationing expenditures.

West Berlin has been an exception. To the present, Germany has continued to pay for virtually all local services and facilities needed by allied troops stationed there. In the case of the U.S. brigade in West Berlin, the value of these services is almost $40 million a year.[3]

Total U.S. expenditures on military facilities, local services, construction, and locally purchased supplies for U.S. forces in Western Europe are estimated at about $1 billion for 1971. Somewhat more than half of this amount will be spent in Germany and $300 million in the other industrial member countries of NATO. The remaining $200 million will be spent in the poorer NATO countries (Greece, Turkey, Portugal), or on NATO infrastructure projects, or in non-NATO countries (France, Spain, and Switzerland). Estimated U.S. expenditures in each country for 1971 are shown below.*

Country	Estimated U.S. expenditure (millions of dollars)
Germany	550
United Kingdom	125
Italy	65
Netherlands	35
Denmark	30
Belgium	20
Norway	10
Subtotal	835
Other NATO countries (Greece, Turkey, Portugal)	75
Other Western European countries (France, Spain, Switzerland)	45
Unallocated	75
Total	1,030

These expenditures are incurred principally for the maintenance and operation of U.S. bases in Europe, through direct employment of foreign citizens in Europe, through payments to foreign contractors, or through the local expenditures of U.S. contractors. For example, at least two-thirds of the total is spent on a variety of operating services, including communications, utilities, and the maintenance and repair of military property and equipment.[4] A smaller proportion is spent for construction, supplies, and miscellaneous purposes.

New arrangements under which Europeans might absorb some of these costs presumably would be limited to the industrial member countries of NATO. U.S. expenditures for local military services,

* Data are from Table 5-5, p. 129.

facilities, and supplies in this group of countries would cover more than $800 million of the total. One attractive approach to a change in arrangements, given the character of these expenditures, would consist in transforming U.S. military bases in Europe into allied bases, from which a change in cost sharing would logically follow. Such arrangements might include the following elements. The United States could transfer to the host country title to all construction and base equipment, thus relinquishing in advance any U.S. claims for reimbursement for such assets when its forces leave. In addition, the United States could agree to provide specified categories of replacement equipment for these bases in the future, to serve allied as well as American forces. In return, the host country would undertake to provide the local services necessary to maintain and operate the base.

As part of such an approach, and in the absence of appreciable military constraints, allied units could be brought into U.S. bases and small U.S. units, now separately based, could be consolidated into large allied installations.

NATO has already begun to move in this direction. Some training areas in Germany are now used jointly by the NATO nations with forces in Central Europe; U.S. Air Force elements are being maintained at six West German bases; and a missile firing range in the Mediterranean has been funded by NATO and jointly used for several years. Joint basing could be greatly expanded, with beneficial consequences for collective defense, and could eventually become the general practice.

Arrangements would be bilateral and could vary from country to country, but the principle of joint basing would serve as a politically useful NATO-wide framework in which to negotiate a change in cost-sharing responsibilities. In effect, some of our NATO allies would assume the cost of a substantial part of the local services for which the United States now pays. If as a result the alliance were strengthened for the long term, they would receive in return greater assurance of American participation in Western Europe's defense and thereby a greater sense of military security, as well as contractual benefits in the form of clear title to the bases and facilities.

In sum, European cost sharing could provide budgetary benefits for the United States. If negotiated on the basis of agreed principles covering the indefinite future, it could remove some serious irritants in current arrangements, both within the United States and between the United States and its European allies, and could improve the effectiveness of collective defense arrangements. Moreover, this form of budgetary savings for the United States would equally help the balance of payments, as discussed below. These are important benefits, and moves in this direction may well be politically essential on both sides of the Atlantic. As in the case of most economy measures, however, the amounts involved under any conceivable arrangements would be very small in relation to the total budget cost of our NATO forces and therefore would leave unresolved the issue of whether the United States can or should bring about a significant shift in budget priorities by reducing its NATO commitment.

DUAL BASING U.S. FORCES. Can savings be made by bringing back forces from Europe but prepositioning part or all of their equipment in Europe and providing airlift capacity for rapid return in the event of an emergency? This technique was used in 1968, when two-thirds of a division was rotated to the United States as part of Operation Reforger. The Air Force counterpart, called Crested Cap, involved dual basing of four tactical squadrons. The experience to date indicates that such moves can save in foreign exchange but promise little saving in the budget.

The major recurring savings from dual basing come from economizing on moving troops and dependents between the United States and Europe on completion of tours of duty and from reduced pipeline and storage costs for supplies and equipment. But dual basing also involves some increased costs. Civilians in the United States must be employed at higher salaries to replace the European civilians employed when the troops were in Europe. In addition, one-time costs must be incurred to bring men and supplies back, to prepare and store the equipment left in Europe, to build or put back into operation base and housing facilities for the units returned to the United States, and to buy training equipment to replace the equipment prepositioned in Europe.

Defense Department data from the 1968 redeployment exercise suggest that dual basing of one division would incur one-time costs of $120 million and produce annual budget savings of $60 million.[5] Balance-of-payments savings, after initial costs, could amount to $100 million a year.[6]

As a guide to any future redeployments, however, these figures probably understate costs and overstate annual savings. They do not allow for constructing new facilities or reopening bases in the United States, or for hiring additional U.S. civilians. Such costs were not necessary in 1968, when there was a relatively small rotation and a substantial number of unused base facilities in the United States resulting from deployments to Vietnam. For a very much larger rotation, however, possibilities for such savings would be far more limited, particularly if surplus military bases in the United States were to be closed down. Taking these factors into account, one-time costs are likely to be higher and annual savings lower than the experience from Operation Reforger would suggest.

In any case, the calculations depend heavily on the assumptions used regarding the amount of equipment prepositioned in Europe, the availability of fast sea transport, and the speed desired for returning the troops to Europe. The rough calculations in Table 5-2 indicate the wide range of possibilities. For example, in Option 1, if the entire equipment of a division redeployed to the United States were prepositioned in Europe, it would be necessary to purchase an additional set of equipment for the division to use for training while it was in the United States. On the other hand, it might not be necessary to provide for much additional airlift capacity. Without additional airlift requirements, one-time costs per redeployed division might come to $370 million, and annual operating costs would remain about the same as they would be for a division stationed in Europe. In an emergency, the division could be returned to Europe with perhaps an acceptable amount of delay, but when forces and equipment are separated, there is the risk that the equipment may not be available at the right time and place—or even at all, if the area where it is stored has been overrun.

TABLE 5-2. *Estimated Costs and Savings in Redeploying a Division from Europe and Dual Basing It in the United States*

Millions of dollars

Calculations and options	One-time cost (+) or saving (−)	Annual cost (+) or saving (−)
Initial calculations[a]		
Movement to United States	+30	
Reduced need for change of station moves		−45
Employing U.S. instead of foreign civilians		+25
Reduced pipeline and storage costs	−30	−20
Closing facilities in Europe	+10	−5
Providing facilities in United States	+60	+5
Net cost or saving	+70	−40
Option 1: All equipment except aircraft prepositioned in Europe; no additional airlift required		
Maintenance cost for equipment in Europe		+40
Equipment purchased in United States to replace prepositioned equipment in Europe	+300	
Option 2: No equipment prepositioned in Europe; additional airlift required		
Cost of capacity to airlift division and equipment:		
By M+30 (24 C-5As)	+600	+140
By M+15 (56 C-5As)	+1,400	+340
Option 3: No equipment prepositioned in Europe; return by M+90 with existing airlift and sealift		
Net cost or saving	+70	−40

Sources: Estimates based on data appearing in the testimony of General Earle G. Wheeler in *Department of Defense Appropriations for Fiscal Year 1969*, Hearings before the Senate Committee on Appropriations, 90 Cong. 2 sess. (1968), Pt. 5, pp. 2669–70; *Military Construction Appropriations for 1970, Pt. 2: Department of the Air Force and Department of the Army*, Hearings before a Subcommittee of the House Committee on Appropriations, 91 Cong. 1 sess. (1969), Pt. 2, pp. 279–80; Department of the Air Force; and testimony of Lieutenant General George S. Boylan in *Military Airlift*, Hearings before the Subcommittee on Military Airlift of the House Committee on Armed Services, 91 Cong. 2 sess. (1970), p. 6664.

a. These calculations are based on the redeployment of only one division. Redeployment of additional divisions could more than proportionately increase costs, largely because of the need to cope with greater transportation bottlenecks at the terminals as the load increased.

Alternatively, as in Option 2, the equipment could remain with the division, with reliance on additional airlift capacity to return both men and equipment to Europe rapidly at a time of crisis. In this case, there would be no need to buy an additional set of equipment, but the cost of buying and operating additional airlift capacity would overwhelm all other cost considerations. Calculations for this option assume that the C-5A air transport program, to be completed in 1973, will provide the capacity to airlift forces now in the United States that are earmarked for Europe. Additional airlift capacity would therefore be necessary for the rapid return of divisions brought back from Europe for dual basing in the United States, and such capacity would be extraordinarily expensive.

Or, as in Option 3, men and equipment could be returned to the United States, and planning could proceed on the assumption that they would not need to return to Europe until perhaps ninety days after mobilization. In this case reliance could be placed mainly on sealift capacity, which in that period could probably be mobilized on an emergency basis without excessive cost. One-time costs then would be low—perhaps $70 million—and annual operating savings per division would amount to perhaps $40 million. In this period of time, however, the military crisis could occur and be over before these forces could be returned to Europe. This evident possibility might have unfortunate effects on both the Western European will to maintain an adequate defense and on Soviet assessments of the costs and risks of applying military pressure. Therefore, any dual-basing arrangements should provide for the rapid return of forces if NATO is to be maintained in anything like its present form.

These assumptions and cost estimates are highly arbitrary. The most practical options would involve some mixture of prepositioned equipment in Europe and provision for additional airlift capacity. Nevertheless, the calculations shown in Table 5-2 provide strong enough grounds to conclude that in almost any foreseeable circumstances, the cost of assuring the rapid return of a redeployed division to Europe would be very high.

In short, bringing back troops from Europe and restationing them at U.S. bases cannot in itself save much, if any, budget money. It costs about the same to maintain a division force in Europe as it does in the United States. To be sure, the 227,000 military dependents[7] in Europe and the 14,000 American civilians serving with U.S. forces in Europe cost money—but no more than they would at home. Family allowances are about the same. In fact, they might increase because government-furnished housing for dependents is already in place in Europe, but more would be needed at U.S. bases if the troops were returned; and there is no reason to assume that the number of civilian employees would be reduced if the forces were stationed in the United States. At the maximum, and disregarding the effects on NATO, bringing back *all* forces from Europe and stationing them in the United States for return to Europe in an emergency would save perhaps $200 million to $300 million a year (while involving large one-time investment costs). The possibility of such annual savings would quickly disappear if Europeans shared more in the cost of operating NATO bases.

Dual basing for U.S. NATO forces would substantially increase budget costs if airlift capacity were built to return them rapidly to Europe in an emergency. Even with additional airlift, there would be a reduction in military capability—namely, the availability of the division to NATO fifteen to thirty days later than it would be available if it remained in Europe. The alternative of no additional airlift implies a far greater reduction in military capability, since the redeployed division probably could not return to Europe before sixty days.

The only way to effect large budget savings in military expenditures for NATO, therefore, is to deactivate troops assigned to NATO or oriented to meet European contingencies—whether they are stationed in Europe or in the United States. In other words, saving money depends not on reducing force levels in Europe but on reducing the total U.S. force structure. How U.S. troops for NATO fit into this structure is examined below.

Total U.S. Budget Costs for NATO

Considerably less than half of the total U.S. forces maintained for European contingencies are actually in Europe. Stationed or based in the United States are the equivalent of five active division forces, six reserve divisions, ten active tactical air wings, seven reserve air wings, two carrier task forces, and other units, all earmarked for or oriented to European contingencies. Taking into account the cost of these forces as well as those stationed in Europe, and adding allowances for such costs as intelligence and communications, training, central supply, retirement pay, and administration, the cost of the U.S. force contribution to European defense in fiscal 1972 is estimated at approximately $25 billion.[8] This figure is essentially a numerical description of a force-planning concept; it is not an unequivocal estimate of the U.S. military investment in the defense of Europe or a statement of the *incremental* cost of such an investment. Understood in these terms, such cost estimates can be a useful analytical tool. A breakdown is shown in Table 5-3.

Viewed in this manner, U.S. forces for European contingencies make up more than half the total U.S. baseline or peacetime general purpose force structure, that is, excluding incremental forces and costs for Vietnam. The primary missions of these general purpose forces are to protect the United States and its overseas interests and commitments and to deter conflicts. Although the extent of these interests and commitments is open to interpretation, force planning must be based in part on assigning priorities and weights among them and on assessing risks and possible losses that would arise from contingencies in various geographic regions of the world. Expenditures for these general purpose forces in fiscal 1972 are estimated at approximately $50 billion. Table 5-4 shows an estimated apportionment of forces and costs by geographic contingency, comparing forces planned for contingencies in Europe with forces planned for contingencies in Asia and in other areas (such as the Western Hemisphere) and with forces in the strategic reserve.

These data make somewhat more manageable the analysis of the budget issues and choices raised by U.S. military spending on forces for European contingencies. Assuming that severe constraints will be imposed on the military budget throughout the 1970s, the possibilities for savings can be examined in terms of a simplified range of options for the general purpose force structure as a whole. Indeed, this is the

TABLE 5-3. *Estimated Cost of U.S. General Purpose Forces for NATO and European Contingencies, by Region, Fiscal Year 1972*

Costs in millions of dollars

	Units		
Region and force	In Europe	In United States	Total cost
Central region[a]			
Army divisions			
Active	$4\frac{1}{3}$	$3\frac{2}{3}$	8,250
Reserve	...	6	2,100
Air Force tactical wings			
Active	7	9	5,650
Reserve	...	$7\frac{1}{3}$	750
Antisubmarine and antiair warfare forces			
(percent of total)[b]	*10*	*25*	2,300
Airlift and sealift forces (percent of total)[b]	...	*50*	600
Subtotal			19,650
Southern region[a]			
Marine active divisions/wings	1/9	8/9	1,050
Navy active carrier task forces	2	2	2,600
Antisubmarine and antiair warfare forces			
(percent of total)[b]	*5*	*10*	1,000
Amphibious and other naval forces			
(percent of total)[b]	7	26	1,100
Subtotal	...	...	5,750
Total	...	...	25,400

Sources: Charles L. Schultze and others, *Setting National Priorities: The 1972 Budget* (Brookings Institution, 1971), p. 55; statement of Secretary of Defense Melvin R. Laird in *Department of Defense Appropriations for 1971*, Hearings before a Subcommittee of the House Committee on Appropriations, 92 Cong. 2 sess. (1970), Pt. 1, p. 270; statement of General Leonard F. Chapman, Jr., Commandant of the Marine Corps, ibid., p. 740; testimony of Admiral Thomas H. Moorer in *CVAN-70 Aircraft Carrier*, Joint Hearings before the Joint Senate-House Armed Services Subcommittee of the Senate and House Armed Services Committees, 91 Cong. 2 sess. (1970), p. 135; *The Military Balance, 1970–71* (London: Institute for Strategic Studies, 1970), pp. 3–5; statement of William W. Kaufmann in *Changing National Priorities*, Hearings before the Subcommittee on Economy in Government of the Joint Economic Committee, 91 Cong. 2 sess (1970), Pt. 1, p. 211.

a. The distribution of forces between NATO's central and southern regions reflects their primary mission and/or likely deployment in a NATO contingency. However, the nature of general purpose forces is such that they could be deployed differently, depending on the nature of a particular contingency. Planning for central region forces, for example, also contemplates their use in northern region contingencies.

b. In U.S. force structure; excludes escorts for attack carriers.

TABLE 5-4. *Possible Distribution and Estimated Costs of Proposed General Purpose Forces by Geographic Contingency, Fiscal Year 1972*

Costs in billions of dollars

Type of force	Europe	Asia	Other areas	Strategic reserve	Total
Active Army and Marine divisions	9	4	1	2⅓	16⅓
National Guard and reserve divisions	6	...	...	3	9
Navy attack carrier task forces[a]	4	6	1	2	13
Marine air wings	1	2	...	...	3
Air Force tactical wings	16	5	...	...	21
Total cost	25.4	15.6	1.7	4.6	50.9[b]

Sources: Charles L. Schultze and others, *Setting National Priorities: The 1972 Budget* (Brookings Institution, 1971), p. 54; Defense Report: A Statement by Secretary of Defense Melvin R. Laird, *Fiscal Year 1971, Defense Program and Budget,* before a Joint Session of the Senate Armed Services and Appropriations Committees (U.S. Government Printing Office, 1970), pp. 138–40; statement of William W. Kaufmann in *Changing National Priorities,* Hearings before the Subcommittee on Economy in Government of the Joint Economic Committee, 91 Cong. 2 sess. (1970), Pt. 1, p. 211.

a. All attack carriers on station (two in the Atlantic, three in the Pacific) and their immediate backup carriers are allocated to Europe and Asia.

b. Includes $3.7 billion for research and development costs not allocated by geographic contingencies.

only useful way of looking at the problem. Consideration of whether budget savings are possible by redeploying forces from Europe must be related to the size and character of the total force structure envisaged.

WHAT WOULD SAVINGS MEAN? The first question to examine is the priorities assigned to U.S. forces for Europe in the current force structure. This structure, as projected in the budget for fiscal 1972 and in the President's 1971 Foreign Policy Message to the Congress, reflects the basic reassessment of force planning strategy undertaken by the Nixon administration over the past two years. Throughout the 1960s, U.S. force planning under the "two and one-half war" strategy was based on an assumed need to deal simultaneously with the initial phases of major conventional attacks in Europe and Asia, along with a minor contingency elsewhere. The current force structure is explicitly based on a "one and one-half war" strategy in which the size of general purpose forces is determined by the requirement to deal with the initial phase of a major attack either in Europe or in Asia, but not simultaneously in both. As a result of this shift in strategy, the number of active divisions (Army plus Marine) was reduced from nineteen and one-third in the pre-Vietnam baseline force to sixteen and one-third, as projected in the budget for fiscal 1972, along with somewhat more modest reductions in attack carrier forces and in Air Force tactical air wings.

These cuts are being made without affecting the allocation of forces for European contingencies, whether deployed in Europe or in the United States. They will be achieved by deactivating two divisions returning from Vietnam and one division returning from Korea. As is shown in Table 5-4, this will still leave about four divisions, along with high levels of air and naval capabilities, available for and oriented to Asian contingencies—enough to deal with what Secretary of Defense Laird has described as a "subtheater" threat in Asia. But as he pointed out in March 1971, "If a large land war involving the United States should occur in Asia, we would, of course, be prepared to mobilize, and would initially use our non-NATO-committed forces as well as portions of those forces based in the U.S. and earmarked for Asia, if required and feasible, and with emphasis on our air and naval capabilities."[9]

The ground forces projected in the 1972 budget, it may be noted, are about the same size as those maintained during the second Eisenhower administration. At the beginning of 1961, the United States had eleven active combat and three training divisions in the Army, in addition to three active Marine divisions. Of this total force, five divisions were stationed in Europe.

What if budgetary constraints called for a sharper cut in the peacetime force, to achieve a budget saving of perhaps $10 billion while still maintaining the conventional military strength to meet the initial phases of a major contingency either in Europe or in Asia, in line with the "one and one-half war" design? Such a budget might be consistent with keeping in combat-ready status twelve or thirteen active division forces (Army plus Marine), with commensurate naval and air strength.*

One approach to such a budget for general purpose forces would be to concentrate the necessary reduction of about three divisions entirely on forces maintained for Asian contingencies—deactivating virtually all forces returning from Vietnam, the division coming back from Korea, and additional forces now stationed in the United States for possible use in Asia. The estimated annual cost of maintaining forces for possible use in Asia would then be cut drastically from the current level of about $16 billion, but there would still be a significant military force available for a contingency in Asia.†

IMPLICATIONS FOR NATO. A budget cut of this size, approached in this way, would still provide leeway to keep intact the forces available for European contingencies. This distribution of the burden of a significant military budget cut would be consistent with (1) according first priority to maintaining the capability for a graduated response to crises in Europe, (2) encouraging the maintenance of a substantial Western European conventional force capability, and (3) maintaining a U.S. capability to help shape the outcome of Europe's security problems and ultimately its political organization.

These priorities are at least strongly implied by the Nixon doctrine, as elaborated in the President's 1971 Foreign Policy Message. Assisting Asian allies to strengthen their defense capability while reducing the deployment of American forces in the Asian theater would, by extension, argue for budget cuts in the first instance falling most

---

* These force levels would be nominally comparable to the ground strength maintained immediately prior to the Korean war. In 1949, for example, the United States had ten active Army divisions and three Marine divisions, but they were under strength and several were in training. The total military budget in 1949 was about one-third the current level, in constant dollars. At that time, however, the United States clearly dominated in strategic capability.

† Under one version of this alternative, the remaining U.S. force for Asia would include two Marine divisions, one Naval air wing, two Air Force tactical wings, and a large proportion of the antisubmarine warfare and amphibious forces, as well as the strategic airlift and sealift capacity. See the testimony of William W. Kaufmann, *Changing National Priorities*, Hearings before the Subcommittee on Economy in Government of the Joint Economic Committee, 91 Cong. 2 sess. (1970), Pt. 1, p. 211.

heavily on forces maintained for Asian contingencies. Such force-planning priorities are emphasized in Secretary of Defense Laird's 1971 report on the 1972–76 defense program: "With regard to U.S. force capabilities in Asia, we do not plan for the long term to maintain separate large U.S. ground combat forces specifically oriented just to this theater, but we do intend to maintain strong air, naval, and support capabilities."[10]

Suppose nevertheless that the process of cutting the budget for peacetime general purpose forces by $10 billion was approached through a literal interpretation of the "one and one-half war" strategy—that is, by giving equal weight to the threat of major conventional attack in Europe and Asia and to building and maintaining forces that could be used in either theater, thereby lowering sharply the priority now assigned to European contingencies. Would this approach suggest returning to the United States forces now in Europe, so that they could serve as readily for an emergency in Asia as for one in Europe?

At the risk of carrying this artificially simplified analysis too far, it is worthwhile to outline briefly the main elements to consider. Keeping four divisions in Europe would leave about nine divisions in the United States for possible use in Asia or Europe, as well as for a minor contingency elsewhere. If one division is allowed for a minor contingency, eight divisions would remain for a possible crisis in Asia—at least as many as we maintained in peacetime for Asian contingencies under the "two and one-half war" strategy.* Most of these divisions, however, are equipped and trained for use in Europe. To orient them effectively for the two theaters would require stocking additional equipment overseas, more training, and improved readiness techniques. Nothing would be gained under this approach by bringing back part or all of the four divisions deployed in Europe. They would still need to be equipped and trained for a European as well as for an Asian contingency. Moreover, bringing them back, as indicated above, would require some housekeeping investments in the United States

* Whether we continue to deploy one division in Korea does not substantially affect the argument.

and the costly procurement of airlift capacity to make them available for quick return to Europe. In addition, possible repercussions in Western Europe could adversely affect the military balance. When both military and political factors are taken into account, keeping these forces in Europe seems by far the best budgetary bargain.

At what point of budgetary constraint, then, would the "one and one-half war" strategy necessarily require a withdrawal of forces from Europe? There is no simple answer. As total force levels go down, the four divisions in Europe make up a proportionately larger share of the total force structure, with less flexibility in planning and use. For example, at a total force level of ten active divisions, reserves stationed in the United States would probably be too small to meet a major contingency in Asia. Prudence might then suggest the return of some or even all of the divisions from Europe. Not to do so would reflect adherence to a Europe-only strategy for defense against conventional attacks and reliance on nuclear deterrence, local forces, or diplomacy in Asia. On the other hand, given the need for adequate mobilization-day military strength in Europe, bringing back all or a large part of the American forces would necessarily increase reliance on nuclear deterrence in Europe.

Are there other approaches to reducing the U.S. forces allocated for Europe? For example, despite the drawbacks outlined in Chapter 3 and the limitations imposed by the gobal buildup of Soviet naval power, the United States could eliminate one of the two carrier task forces on station in the Mediterranean. On military grounds, such a move would be based on the arguments that carriers in the Mediterranean would be vulnerable to Soviet land-based aircraft in a war involving the USSR and that one carrier task force is sufficient for other contingencies in the Middle East. Even so, the political constraints might be considerable. Substantial reductions in U.S. naval strength in the Mediterranean might have unsettling effects on prospects for political stability in the Middle East. The budgetary consequences, though not major, could be significant: Keeping only one carrier on station in the Mediterranean could result in the deactivation of one to three carriers, depending on alternative requirements for the two backup carriers, with a resultant annual saving of $650 million to $2 billion in the cost of our forces in Europe.

In another approach, European NATO countries might increase their forces on the central front. Each increment of European forces equal to one U.S. division might make possible a reduction of one division in the total U.S. force structure (whether located in the United States or in Europe), at a budgetary saving of $1 billion a year. But where would the additional European forces be found? Chapter 4 treats the political obstacles to increased European defense efforts. France has ruled itself out; Canada, Britain, and the Benelux countries are encountering great difficulty in maintaining their present forces at appropriate quality levels. An Italian division in Central Europe would be a theoretical possibility but would be politically difficult to provide; further, it would create a logistic nightmare, with supply lines either cut off by neutral Austria and Switzerland or too long because of the need to go through France. Germany is the last possibility, and a sizable increase in German forces is probably ruled out by political sensitivities in Western as well as Eastern Europe, whatever the possibilities in the Federal Republic itself.

These considerations are in no sense meant to imply that existing forces—whether for Europe or for Asia and whether stationed abroad or in the United States—could not be organized more effectively and at less cost. The point stressed here is that the way in which U.S. forces for NATO fit into the peacetime structure of general purpose forces and the cost-cutting priorities that emerge from this relationship strongly indicate that, under almost any conceivable force structure alternative, cutting U.S. division strength in Europe would not be likely to produce budget savings and could, in the end, cost more money.

Balance-of-Payments Issues

The foreign exchange costs associated with U.S. forces for NATO raise a different set of issues—logically far less important and seemingly more manageable, but nevertheless an important factor fueling the troop level controversy. The international aspects of the President's economic program of August 15, 1971 could substantially affect the importance of these foreign exchange issues for better or for worse, depending on changes in international monetary arrangements negotiated as a consequence of U.S. suspension of the dollar's convertibility into gold. If these negotiations go badly, the foreign exchange costs associated with NATO could become even more of an irritant than they are now. On the other hand, if they succeed in bringing greater stability to the international monetary system, it may be possible to remove the NATO foreign exchange issue as a factor in U.S.-Western European defense relations. Before considering some of the possibilities, it is worthwhile to examine the character of these costs and past arrangements for dealing with them, particularly as they relate to the financial history of the post-World War II period.

Foreign exchange costs for NATO arise mainly from three categories of expenditures: (1) U.S. payments for local goods and services required to maintain and operate military facilities in Europe, (2) military capital investment in Europe (buildings, equipment, and the U.S. share of NATO infrastructure costs), and (3) local purchases by American military personnel and their dependents stationed in Europe.

Expenditures in the first two categories are made from appropriated funds and are part of the budgetary cost of U.S. forces for NATO (see Table 5-5, below). Expenditures in the third category—personal spending of troops and dependents in the local economy—though derived from appropriated funds (military pay and allowances), are not themselves a budgetary cost but a dollar outlay analogous to the cost of tourism, in this case a kind of automatic or involuntary tourism. All three categories produce windfall foreign exchange receipts for the host country that are related almost entirely to the accident of defense geography and not to competitive economic position. They are, in effect, a reverse form of tied expenditures—tied to purchases abroad rather than at home.

It has become a convention to adjust these foreign exchange expenditures by net receipts from purchases of military equipment by other

NATO countries in the United States. The bulk of these transactions consists of German military purchases in the United States, but most of the other NATO countries also buy U.S. military hardware. In fact, over the years a multilateral trade in military equipment has developed in NATO, including some reverse U.S. military purchases in Canada and Europe.

Assessing the Problem

What constitutes a net foreign exchange flow arising out of NATO is an elusive concept. Disagreements arise in the course of NATO discussions of the foreign exchange problem and of arrangements to deal with it. For one thing, a balance-of-payments cost to the United States from these expenditures does not necessarily mean a foreign exchange gain of the same magnitude to the host country. For example, U.S. military-related expenditures in Germany add to Germany's foreign exchange receipts, but to some degree they also increase Germany's requirements for imported goods and foreign labor. Logically, from Germany's point of view, some adjustment should be made in U.S. foreign exchange costs to arrive at Germany's net windfall in foreign exchange receipts. From the American point of view, apart from any German imports from the United States induced by these military expenditures, the foreign exchange cost is still there—wherever the benefits ultimately accrue.*

Analogous arguments on the receipt side of the ledger apply to U.S. foreign exchange gains from sales of military equipment to Germany and other NATO countries. To the degree that such sales would be made in any event, as was largely the case during the period when Germany was rebuilding its military forces, they do not represent a true offset to U.S. foreign exchange costs for NATO.

* Other more complex arguments are raised. For example, is this military-related spending to be viewed as a net addition to demand in the host country and a net subtraction from demand in the troop-sending country? Or is it to be assumed that in the absence of this spending, government policy would have ensured the same level of employment? In the first case, the net foreign exchange consequences would be less than the nominal amounts; in the second, they would be more nearly the same.

TABLE 5-5. *Estimated Foreign Exchange Outlays Associated with U.S. Forces in Europe, 1971*

Millions of dollars

Category of U.S. foreign exchange expenditure or receipt	Germany	U.K.	Italy	Netherlands	Denmark	Belgium	Norway	Subtotal	Other NATO[a]	Other W. Europe[b]	Unallocated	Total
Operation and maintenance of military facilities and other U.S. military expenditures in Europe on equipment and services	550	125	65	35	30	20	10	835	75	45	75	1,030
Local expenditures of U.S. military and civilian personnel and dependents	600	125	50	15	5	20	...	815	35	50	...	900
Subtotal	1,150	250	115	50	35	40	10	1,650	110	95	75	1,930
Less foreign purchases of U.S. military equipment	450[c]	125	50	15	...	10	...	650	...	...	...	650
Net U.S. foreign exchange cost	700	125	65	35	35	30	10	1,000	110	95	75[d]	1,280

Sources: Estimates based on data for U.S. defense expenditures in Western Europe by country, supplied by the U.S. Department of Commerce for 1970 and appearing for earlier years in Cora E. Shepler and Leonard C. Campbell, "United States Defense Expenditures Abroad," *Survey of Current Business*, Vol. 49 (December 1969), pp. 40–47; "North Atlantic Assembly Draft Report on Burden Sharing and the Economic Aspects of the Common Defense Effort," prepared by Senator Charles H. Percy, U.S. Rapporteur, Exhibit 1, *Congressional Record*, daily ed., July 10, 1970, p. S11066; testimony of Principal Deputy Assistant Secretary of Defense (Comptroller) Don R. Brazier before the Subcommittee on International Exchanges and Payments of the Joint Economic Committee, *Congressional Record*, daily ed., June 30, 1971, pp. S10319–21. All figures are rounded. Data appearing in the North Atlantic Assembly Draft Report for fiscal year 1968 are adjusted by change in U.S. military pay scales for selected countries, with rough estimates for other countries.

a. The low-income countries: Greece, Turkey, and Portugal.

b. France, Switzerland, and Spain.

c. Same level of German military purchases in the United States as in 1970–71 offset agreement, plus allowance of 10 percent to compensate for increased prices.

d. Includes U.S. share of NATO infrastructure expenditures.

For present purposes, it is assumed that such adjustments counterbalance each other, thus permitting the use of gross figures on both the expenditure and receipt sides to arrive at a U.S. foreign exchange balance sheet for NATO activities. There is more than heroics to such a simplifying assumption. Adjustments of gross figures in both directions would be appropriate, but while the possible arguments on amounts are endless, the net change in the balance from such adjustments is not likely to be significant.

Dollar expenditures for these purposes in Western Europe over most of the 1960s stayed fairly consistently at a level of about $1.5 billion a year. The effect of reductions since 1962 in the number of U.S. troops stationed in Europe has generally been offset by price and wage increases. In recent years, however, total expenditures have been rising, principally because of the accelerated increase in U.S. military pay scales, resulting in greater purchases of goods and services by U.S. forces in Europe, and because of the increase in the dollar price of U.S. military purchases of goods and services in Germany resulting from the revaluation of the deutsche mark. Since the relocation of U.S. forces from France in 1967, a growing proportion of these expenditures has been concentrated in Germany.

An approximate projection of the U.S. military foreign exchange balance in Western Europe for 1971 appears in Table 5-5. Gross dollar expenditures are estimated at more than $1.9 billion, of which about $1.7 billion is spent in the European industrial member countries of NATO, with the balance being spent in Greece, Turkey, and nonmember countries, or on unallocated expenditures such as those for NATO infrastructure. Net foreign exchange expenditures in the industrial member countries of NATO, after transactions in military equipment, are estimated at $1 billion. Germany accounts for 70 percent of this total.

No provision was made in NATO, at its formation, to deal with this inherent maldistribution of foreign exchange expenditures simply because it was viewed as a useful balance-of-payments adjustment measure rather than as a problem. U.S. policy in fact sought to maximize dollar expenditures in Europe.

Until 1955, Germany paid for the local currency cost of U.S. forces stationed there, but expenditures of U.S. troops and their dependents in Germany, as well as all dollar expenditures elsewhere in NATO, were not covered. Throughout NATO's first decade, U.S. forces were a large and regular source of European foreign exchange earnings. In addition, the United States provided grants of about $13 billion in military equipment and supplies to European NATO countries, including Germany, to help them build defense capabilities without unduly burdening either their foreign exchange reserves or their budgets. This relationship continued for too long a period, largely because of a cultural lag regarding the "dollar shortage." When concern began to arise abroad about the continued deficits in the U.S. balance of payments, one reaction in the United States was to examine the balance-of-payments effects of all U.S. government programs abroad in search of possible savings in foreign exchange outlays. Military expenditures in Europe gained immediate attention in that examination.

The issue of foreign exchange costs came to a head at the end of 1960, so far as U.S.-German relations were concerned, and the confrontation resulted in a series of formal offset arrangements from 1961 on. The first group of offsets (1961–66) consisted of German purchases of U.S. military equipment, or advance payments for such equipment, to the full amount of U.S. foreign exchange expenditures in Germany. Since German purchases lagged behind U.S. foreign exchange expenditures, these agreements resulted in a substantial buildup of German advance payments to the U.S. Treasury, some of which still have not been spent and on which interest is earned.

The second group (1967–69) consisted of German purchases of a combination of military equipment and medium-term U.S. Treasury securities, along with a German agreement not to convert dollar holdings into gold at the U.S. Treasury. Thus, in acknowledgment of Germany's inability to buy military equipment to the full amount of U.S. foreign exchange costs, the purchase of special medium-term U.S. government securities was substituted for German advance payments to the U.S. Treasury and, far more important, Germany through its agreement to hold dollars rather than gold took on what amounted to an obligation to help finance a possible U.S. deficit whenever and to the full extent that its own payments position was in surplus.

In the agreement ending June 30, 1971, the major change was a German undertaking to buy ten-year U.S. government securities at approximately half the market rate of interest and some U.S. Export-Import Bank and Marshall Plan loans to other countries, instead of buying U.S. medium-term securities at commercial interest rates.*

Germany continued to observe its agreement not to ask the U.S. Treasury to convert dollar holdings into gold. As a result, approximately $4 billion in dollar assets were added to its reserves in 1970, as well as additional amounts in 1971. Germany's willingness to add dollars to its reserves on this scale has been an important constructive factor in the operation of the international monetary system during the period of intermittent crises from 1967 to 1971.

Negotiations for the 1972–73 offset agreement, which were not completed when the previous agreement expired, reportedly introduced some promising new elements. According to press reports, the next two-year agreement, in addition to German military purchases in the United States and German long-term loans to the United States at less than market rates of interest, will include a German payment of $98 million for the renovation of American barracks and airfields in Germany and "direct cash payments to the American government" totaling about $218 million over the next two years.[11]

Elsewhere in NATO Europe, the United States has been able to do

---

* Some of the technical differences among U.S.-German agreements had important consequences. In the 1967–69 agreements, the German Central Bank purchased U.S. government securities and treated them as reserves since, by agreement, they could be redeemed before maturity if German reserves fell below a specified level. Early redemption did occur in 1969, when Germany lost a large volume of reserves following the revaluation of the mark. To gain dollars for use at that time, the Central Bank sold $500 million of gold to the U.S. Treasury out of its total gold stock of some $4.5 billion. Rather than sell more gold, it chose to redeem $500 million of these offset securities, as it was entitled to do under the agreement. This action raised questions in the minds of members of the Congress who closely follow this issue and are skeptical about the value of this form of offset. In the 1970–71 agreement, the German government, not the Central Bank, purchased the securities, presumably from appropriated funds. The securities do not have an early redemption clause.

no more than make catch-as-catch-can arrangements combining purchases of U.S. military equipment and medium-term U.S. Treasury securities.

Although past measures were perhaps a necessary stopgap as part of a transitional process, they are no longer tenable and cannot meet the political and financial requirements for a strong and lasting U.S.-European defense relationship. Two major deficiencies are evident.

First, past measures did not succeed in automatically neutralizing NATO foreign exchange expenditures as a political issue. Their failure to do so has fostered a belief in the United States that something must be done about these expenditures, and hence about troops in Europe, in order to "save the dollar." In turn, this belief, and an associated feeling of resentment that inequities are involved, threatens to influence on the wrong grounds the definition of U.S. security interests.

Second, past measures permitted NATO to exert a perverse effect on the international monetary system. The United States and Britain, the major deficit countries, consistently suffered foreign exchange losses from their NATO obligations, while Germany and other European surplus countries consistently received balance-of-payments gains from NATO. The disturbing effect of these NATO-induced foreign exchange flows on the international monetary system were mitigated by Germany's cooperation in holding dollar reserves, thereby providing a stable means of financing U.S. balance-of-payments deficits, and more recently by German revaluations of the mark. However, this cooperation did not receive the political credit it deserved in the United States, and it could create political problems in Germany when dollar reserves rose dramatically, as was evidenced by some rather heated arguments over which country was to blame for the international financial crisis of May 1971.

These two deficiencies would disappear if a fully efficient and politically neutral process existed to adjust chronic surpluses and deficits among the industrial countries. There would be little reason for the United States to be concerned about military or other government expenditures abroad *on balance-of-payments grounds* if the international system were such that (1) the U.S. balance-of-payments position tended toward equilibrium without exercising constraints on U.S. domestic employment policies, or (2) the financing of U.S. deficits did not give rise to political tensions in the surplus countries or provide arguments for the adoption of restrictive policies in the United States. Until this happy state of affairs is achieved, it is politically essential that foreign exchange flows arising out of NATO should help rather than hinder the adjustment process.

Possible Improvements

With broader cost sharing for base operations and with new foreign exchange ground rules, the elements of the present arrangement could readily be developed into a workable system for the long term.

As is indicated in Table 5-5, U.S. foreign exchange expenditures associated with American forces in the industrial member countries of NATO amount to about $1.7 billion a year, including the U.S. share of NATO infrastructure projects. It is assumed here that U.S. foreign exchange expenditures elsewhere in Europe, amounting to approximately $200 million and incurred principally in Greece, Turkey, and Spain, would not be covered by special cost sharing and foreign exchange offsets.

COST SHARING. Arrangements whereby the host country in effect assumed the major part of the local cost of operating, maintaining, and constructing U.S. military facilities could considerably reduce the dimensions of the foreign exchange problem—and, even more important, could answer U.S. complaints of inequities in the existing system. For example, if approximately two-thirds of present U.S. local costs for military bases and related services became the responsibility of the host country, U.S. foreign exchange outlays and budget costs for NATO would be reduced by $500 million. Rather than seeking a fixed amount to be periodically renegotiated, it would be far preferable, politically and perhaps militarily as well, to work toward joint basing arrangements with host country cost sharing built in, as described earlier in this chapter. Thus, Britain as well as the United

States would receive net benefits, an arrangement that is consistent with current political requirements for maintaining a steady position on force levels in Europe. Costs would be concentrated in Germany, but other countries on the Continent with NATO bases would share in them. The system as a whole would have the advantage of being multilateral in character and based on negotiated principles designed to continue for the duration of NATO.

Two common arguments against cost sharing are that (1) it involves a budgetary problem among European countries that is either unmanageable or likely to result in an equivalent reduction in needed expenditures on their own forces, and that (2) it would be viewed in Germany as a return to occupation cost arrangements and therefore would be politically unpalatable. Concerning the first argument, a shift of $500 million in local support costs, while significant, would be a relatively small adjustment; it would represent an increase of about 2 percent in the defense budgets of the European member countries of NATO and a virtually negligible proportion of their total budgetary expenditures. With regard to the second argument, the total amount involved may be contrasted with German expenditures of $900 million in 1952 for local services to U.S. forces, which at current prices and exchange rates would cost roughly $1.5 billion. This large difference in itself distinguishes this kind of cost sharing from occupation costs. Joint basing arrangements would set them even further apart.

The only guidelines to cost sharing are that it should cover a substantial part of the foreign exchange problem and adequately deal with the equity argument—that local military base costs, or at least the predominant portion, should not be borne by the country that sends and pays for the forces. Beyond this, the outcome depends on politics and good sense on both sides of the Atlantic and on recognition by both the United States and Western Europe that the importance of mutual security interests and the large cost of the forces themselves, which are not under contention, dwarf possible negotiating differences on this issue.

PROVIDING OFFSETS. If local support costs were shared as suggested above, U.S. foreign exchange costs for NATO would amount to approximately $1.2 billion a year. A NATO-wide agreement explicitly tying offsets to the balance-of-payments adjustment process could effectively neutralize foreign exchange costs as a factor in U.S. security decisions—or in the decisions of other NATO countries stationing troops outside their borders for alliance purposes. Agreement on two operating rules would meet these requirements:

1. Any NATO country incurring foreign exchange costs as a consequence of stationing forces in any other NATO country would have those costs offset through actions taken by the host country.

2. However, in any given year, the host country's obligation would automatically be waived if the country stationing forces abroad were in balance-of-payments equilibrium or surplus.

Such NATO-wide rules would apply most importantly to ways of dealing with U.S. foreign exchange costs and German foreign exchange receipts arising out of NATO. These two flows are by far the largest part of the total. The rules would apply equally to British net deficits arising out of NATO and to the relatively small net foreign exchange receipts that other industrial member countries receive from NATO activities.

Three related methods of providing offsets could be used within this framework:

1. Offsetting purchases of military equipment would be the principal means, as is now the case. The logic of this course is strongly based on economic considerations. U.S. comparative advantages as a supplier of military hardware are obviously very great. In an environment of free trade in military hardware, American exports to Western Europe would be a great deal larger than they are now.

The potential market in Europe is sufficiently large for the purpose. For example, in the United States, procurement accounts for about 30 percent of the defense budget. If soft goods and such items as ammunition and military vehicles, where technology is not a significant factor, are excluded, the proportion might be approximately 25 percent. Applying this proportion to European NATO countries suggests a market for military hardware of about $1.25 billion in Germany[12] and about $4 billion in the other NATO countries.

The constraints are political. Each country wants its own defense industry, has its own defense industry pressures, and believes more or less strongly in the mystique of technological spinoff from defense production. Furthermore, at least in theory, large purchases of military equipment from the United States could impose limits on Europe-wide cooperation in defense production. In fact, the total market is probably large enough for both cooperative European defense projects and large-scale military purchases in the United States, including purchases of American components for use in European joint production. Security factors are also involved: How much dependence on defense production in other countries constitutes "excessive" dependence? In the absence of these constraints, it is probably safe to conclude that Germany's net purchases in the United States would offset a major part of its NATO foreign exchange receipts. Other European NATO countries gaining foreign exchange could easily provide full offsets—and more—in military purchases, with clear economic advantage to themselves.

In any event, military purchases made as offsets should be negotiated under relatively relaxed conditions. Specifically, such arrangements should not directly put pressure on European countries to buy U.S. military equipment and certainly no pressure to buy at anything but a clear saving over domestic cost; and they should not stand in the way of European cooperation in military production.

2. A second offset category could be deferred military purchases. If, because of domestic constraints, a country chose not to buy enough military equipment in the United States to meet its offset obligation on a current basis, it could make up the balance by paying for a claim on U.S. military equipment to be exercised over the indefinite future. A claim of this kind could be represented by a special noninterest-bearing financial instrument. This is essentially what Germany did during the first offset agreements, when it made advance payments to the U.S. Treasury to cover the difference between its offset obligation and the value of the U.S. military equipment it had on order but had not received (or that it had been unable to order) during the account-

ing period. Because these deposits in the U.S. Treasury earn interest, they have the wrong political connotation. They appear to be German loans to the United States rather than an automatic German offset to an abnormal U.S. outflow. Good alliance politics requires clarity on this central point: that the responsibility for adjustment rests with the country receiving the foreign exchange windfall, unless balance-of-payments positions dictate otherwise.

A financial instrument representing a claim against military equipment purchased in the future could be made more flexible if it could be used for other purposes by agreement of the two governments. Such other uses presumably would meet the test of additionality—that they resulted in an addition to U.S. foreign exchange receipts or substituted for U.S. foreign exchange expenditures that otherwise would have occurred. (Examples might be German expenditures in the United States for a joint space project or German NATO-oriented assistance to Greece or Turkey that substituted for American assistance.) This financial instrument could gain reserve status if it could be used freely for any purpose whenever the holder's other international reserves were used up. In effect, it would become a reserve asset that would be put at the bottom of the reserve pile—to be drawn on after gold, special drawing rights (SDRs), and foreign exchange holdings were exhausted. This arrangement would ease the host country's financing problem, because a financial claim against future receipt of U.S. military equipment that also qualified as a reserve asset could be treated as such by the central bank and would not have to be financed through budgetary appropriations until it was used.*

It is conceivable, but only in the case of Germany, that the accumulation of claims for deferred military purchases from the United States could become embarrassingly large. This possibility would be

---

* As an advance deposit, such payments would improve U.S. balance-of-payments accounts on both the liquidity and official settlements basis. Treated as a reserve asset, these payments would help only the liquidity definition of U.S. financial accounts. From the U.S. point of view, this distinction should carry no weight if provisions that could make it possible to treat such an instrument as a reserve asset are helpful and perhaps necessary in building a workable offset system.

remote if Germany maintained even its current level of military purchases from the United States.* Should the accumulation become too large, however, the burden would be on Germany to make the necessary adjustments by revising its procurement policies or buying more military hardware from the United States.

3. Alternatively, the accumulation of claims might accompany a chronic German or European Community surplus position that called for currency revaluation on both domestic and international grounds. Such action by Germany alone or with its Community partners would contribute to balance-of-payments equilibrium for the United States. Should the United States achieve equilibrium, it would lose its offset rights for that year and Germany could draw down its accumulation of deferred purchase claims to pay for any military equipment it might wish to buy. In this sense, a currency revaluation or other action to eliminate a chronic balance-of-payments surplus would become indirectly a third category of offset—one that would acquire added importance if reform of the international monetary system made possible more frequent changes in exchange rates.†

RELATED PROPOSALS. It may be useful to compare such a system with other recent proposals to deal with various aspects of the NATO foreign exchange flows, notably the recommendations of Senator Charles H. Percy and the package offered by the European NATO countries at the December 1970 NATO ministerial meeting.

* For example, total U.S. military-related foreign exchange expenditures in Germany are estimated at $1.2 billion in 1971. Assuming German cost-sharing payments of $400–$450 million for U.S. military facilities in Germany, as well as German purchases of military equipment of $450 million, financial claims against future military purchases would be accumulated at the rate of $300–$350 million a year—or perhaps $3 billion over a decade, assuming the continued persistence of German surpluses. In comparison, German reserves have recently averaged about $10 billion and are currently much higher because of the continued presence of speculative funds from abroad.

† Two related problems need special comment. One is the technical question of defining a country's balance-of-payments position and hence its offset responsibilities. The concept of a basic deficit or surplus—that is, balance on current account plus the balance on long-term capital account—would seem most appropriate and least subject to juggling. The second is the question where responsibility would lie if Germany, as a result of revaluation, moved into a balance-of-payments deficit while the United States was also in a deficit position. Some negotiated sharing of responsibility would then seem both sensible and workable.

Senator Percy's proposals are similar in a number of important respects to those outlined above. They were prepared in 1970 in connection with Percy's work as a delegate to the North Atlantic Assembly and are contained in a report on burden sharing submitted by the Assembly's subcommittee on the military balance of payments. They are based on two principles:

A. That local goods and services needed for official use by visiting forces in a NATO country should be paid for as a budget expense by the host country.

B. That other expenditures by visiting forces, including the local currency spending of personnel and dependents, should be paid for in blocked currency for military procurement or other purchases that clearly have an element of additionality.[13]

Applying these principles to the projections shown in Table 5-5 would mean that European NATO members would assume almost $1 billion in local costs now paid by the United States for the maintenance and operation of base facilities in Europe and would buy U.S. military equipment or make advance payments for equipment of about $800 million a year. The result would be automatic neutralization of almost all U.S. foreign exchange costs arising from NATO, as well as a budget saving for the United States that would be significant but still modest in terms of the total cost of the forces maintained for European contingencies.

Senator Percy's proposals contain somewhat stiffer conditions than the system outlined here would entail. Further, they make no provision for U.S. relinquishment of title to base facilities abroad, for joint basing, for the possible use of advance payments as a reserve asset, or for the United States to forgo foreign exchange offsets when its own balance-of-payments position is in equilibrium or surplus. In light of President Nixon's economic policy actions of August 15, 1971, which could bring the U.S. balance of payments into equilibrium fairly rapidly, the last factor could be the most significant.

Another approach stems from the work of the European members of NATO, which have sought since the spring of 1970 to develop a cost-sharing package that would make it easier for the United States to maintain its military forces in Europe. At one stage, the press suggested that Germany was urging, as a first offer, that the Europeans take up approximately $300 million of U.S. local costs in Europe. The explorations took a different tack after October 1970, when President Nixon said during his European visit that the United States would not withdraw its forces unilaterally and indicated that he was looking to the Europeans at least as much for more effective defense arrangements as for financial aid.[14] The outcome was a five-year "defense improvement program" announced by the European NATO members at the ministerial meeting in December 1970. It consists of (1) an allocation of $420 million for NATO infrastructure projects to improve communication and aircraft protection facilities, without any contribution by the United States, and (2) additional European forces costing $450–$500 million over the five-year period.

The total cost of this program to European NATO members would therefore be $200 million a year, or less than 1 percent of what they currently spend on defense. The only financial benefit to the United States would be exemption from sharing the cost of the new infrastructure program. Since the U.S. share for such projects is normally one-third, the saving to the United States would be somewhat less than $30 million a year. No other proposals regarding new financial arrangements were announced after the meeting, suggesting that the ministers made little progress in this area on a NATO-wide basis.

Whatever the merits of one approach or another, the ground rules should clarify the central fact that the offset issue concerns the operation of the international payments system rather than the distribution of real costs within NATO. (This does not apply to the sharing of local support costs, which involves independent equity arguments that must be negotiated and settled on their merits even though the settlement would significantly affect foreign exchange outlays.) A good offset system would facilitate military contributions to NATO by countries fully prepared to assume the resource cost—the cost of equipment, transportation, and troop pay—without real cost to the country providing the offsets. A poor system could jeopardize defense arrangements to no apparent purpose. Neutralizing NATO foreign exchange flows as a factor in military security decisions therefore would seem to be a reasonable and negotiable objective. It should be all the more attainable as exchange rates are realigned and it again becomes realistic to assume that the U.S. balance of payments in the future could as well be in surplus as in deficit. In that event, a U.S. willingness to forgo offsets when its balance of payments is in equilibrium or surplus would be a powerful inducement for European NATO countries to agree to provide full and assured offsets for U.S. NATO foreign exchange costs when the U.S. balance of payments is in deficit.

Broader Issues of Burden Sharing

Collective arrangements become vulnerable when some participants believe that others are not pulling their weight, and the risk of breakdown is greatest if the largest member holds this view. This concern underlies the debate in the Senate on U.S. force levels in Europe. The argument may be summarized as follows: European NATO members should do more in their own defense; if they are not willing to do so, either the United States has an exaggerated view of defense requirements or an outsized view of its security interest in Europe. A further presumption is that if Europeans do more, the United States can do less. Sometimes, because of frustration over past NATO burden-sharing debates, it is believed that European NATO members will realize that they must do more themselves only when shocked into this realization by U.S. force withdrawals.

By some commonly held standards, the American share in European defense arrangements is indeed disproportionately high. Specifically, American forces tend to meet planning goals not only in numbers of units but also in quality, supplies, combat readiness, and mobilization capability. European forces do not. In aggregate terms, the United States spends 7 percent of its gross national product (GNP) on defense, while the European NATO countries spend less than 4 percent. The U.S. defense budget is perhaps three times the combined total defense budgets of all European NATO countries. Of course, the fact that per capita income in the United States is perhaps double the average level in Western Europe suggests a greater U.S. capacity to bear defense burdens. On the other hand, given the geographical area to be defended, these figures indicate slack in the European sector of the NATO system.

Regarding forces on the ground in Europe, the evidence is mixed. Of the immediately available NATO forces, the United States provides only 10 percent of the ground forces, 20 percent of the air forces, and 30 percent of the naval forces. Thus, the defense of Europe is primarily dependent on Europeans. Furthermore, the total cost of the U.S. forces maintained specifically for Europe is less than what is spent by the European NATO countries combined and little more than 2 percent of the U.S. GNP. On the other hand, U.S. forces, because of their nuclear contribution and their state of readiness, are far more important to European defense than the numbers alone suggest.

If one looks at trends, the comparison is not quite so adverse to Europe. In 1969 the United States was spending almost 10 percent of its GNP on defense, compared with 7 percent in 1971, and the trend is still downward. For example, without Vietnam, current U.S. defense spending is about 6 percent of GNP, and this figure may be even lower as a result of post-Vietnam competition for available budgetary resources. On the other hand, European military budgets, while falling moderately as a percent of GNP, have remained fairly constant or have risen slightly (about 2 percent in 1970) in real terms, and this trend may continue in the 1970s. Similarly, during the second half of the 1960s the United States had a considerably larger proportion of its population in the armed forces than did Western Europe. This ratio is changing as the withdrawal of troops from Vietnam continues and U.S. military manpower is reduced. In short, the disparity in military effort between the United States and Europe, while still large, is measurably narrowing.

A look backward also provides a useful perspective. When NATO was formed in 1949, the United States and Western Europe were each spending about 5 percent of GNP on defense. By this standard, the United States, excluding its outlays for Vietnam, is spending about one-fifth too much and Western Europe is spending about one-fifth too little.

The argument is sometimes made that the United States as a world power has wider responsibilities and interests than do the individual European countries and therefore must expect to spend proportionately more on security. A more appropriate comparison, following this line of reasoning, is between the United States and the USSR. While the United States spends 2 percent of GNP on maintaining military forces for European contingencies and 7 percent of GNP for its total military budget, Soviet military outlays are in the area of 10 percent of GNP.

The difficulties with these burden-sharing calculations are inherent in the nature of an alliance involving common security interests and intermingling military and political factors. Carrying such calculations too far risks focusing attention on the wrong questions—whether in terms of costs, security, or politics.

What issues should take priority in the current consideration of NATO burden sharing, and why? The point of this chapter is that since withdrawing forces from Europe in itself would not reduce U.S. defense costs, the first priority in burden sharing should apply to measures that would enable the United States to view its forces stationed in Europe as having financial consequences no different from those of forces stationed in the United States. This would clearly be the case if, as suggested, Western Europe assumed more of the local costs of operating military facilities in Europe and could agree with the United States on rules to insulate the international payments system from the disturbing effects of foreign exchange expenditures arising from NATO force dispositions. Such cost sharing would require an average increase of about 2 percent in the defense budgets of Western European NATO countries. Better foreign exchange rules need entail no real costs and would strengthen the international payments system.

The issue of NATO foreign exchange costs will inevitably enter the bargaining between the United States and Western Europe over the elements of a workable international monetary system following the U.S. suspension of convertibility of the dollar into gold. The danger is that the United States will see these foreign exchange outlays as an expenditure that must be offset in all circumstances, and that Western Europe will believe that changes in the system resulting from American pressure applied unilaterally on August 15, 1971 are a sufficient offset to these costs. Neither attitude would be consistent with the national interests of the United States or Western Europe. Both would benefit from arrangements that treated NATO foreign exchange costs as an element to be used in strengthening the international payments system and not as a resource cost that requires reimbursement.

Satisfactory cost-sharing and foreign exchange offset arrangements would show that the U.S.-Western European defense relationship could last indefinitely—that the United States is prepared to keep its forces in Europe and that Western Europe is prepared to maintain a serious defense effort so long as the need persists. This posture is best calculated, in the end, to permit the kinds of U.S. troop withdrawals from Europe that would achieve real budgetary savings. In the short term, it would facilitate serious consideration within NATO of measures to improve the effectiveness of NATO forces through economies in low-priority military functions, upgrading of combat readiness and mobilization arrangements, and changes in command structure. And in the long term, it would help to convince the USSR that mutual force reduction has advantages; for it would make clear that in the absence of mutual reduction, indefinite continuance of current Western arrangements is more likely than not.

6

Summing Up

THE SIZE AND CHARACTER of American force deployments in Western Europe do not fit a precisely calculable military requirement. How much is enough is not the issue. It is rather how many and what kinds of forces will satisfy a number of considerations, some of them political, others strategic. These considerations should not be seen as immediate or short-term. They have to do rather with the kind of world order the United States seeks to encourage; with the kind of lasting relationship we wish to establish with Western Europe; with how to impart greater stability to the East-West environment while avoiding steps that might encourage latent instabilities.

If the United States is the greatest of modern world powers, it is also among the least experienced, measured by the length of its involvement in world affairs. Since World War II, the United States has been on a learning curve. During this period, we have learned much about leading a collective security system and about nuclear diplomacy.

Predictably, the learning process has been difficult for the leader and the led. As the chief custodian of the West's nuclear as well as nonnuclear power, the United States assumes primary responsibility for the security of a group of less powerful but older societies whose perspective on issues and events is often different from that of their protector. Washington has at times exercised strong—occasionally imaginative—leadership; at other times, of which the present moment is a notable example, it has adopted a more passive view of its unique role in the Western alliance system. Neither the assertive nor the more passive style is free of penalty; each can be relied on to create difficulties. But whatever the virtue of either posture at a given time, what is essential—and sometimes lacking—in the American role is consistency: a reliable sense of proportion, combined with a continuing willingness to fit priorities to basic national interests. Hence, the issue of American troop strength in Europe must be judged both by what is at stake and by changes in the political environment that might justify a revision of U.S. NATO commitments.

At stake is a network of interests and the risk, as distinct from the certainty, that these might be undermined by premature troop withdrawals. Among these interests is security; at critical moments, Americans sense that the integrity of their system relies in some measure on the Western system—on a set of mutually productive relationships between the societies of North America and Western Europe that bear on how they manage their financial, commercial, military, and political affairs. If it should appear that the United States were either unable or unwilling any longer to provide a plausible security guarantee to Western European countries, they might either have to expand their security forces considerably or reach separate understandings with the Soviet Union. The former course would almost certainly require joint Western European arrangements. These might well include a decision to create a separate nuclear deterrent at a time and in circumstances that could lead to political splits likely to destabilize the European unity movement and the Atlantic system as well. Moreover, since the prospect that Western European countries could deploy jointly controlled defense forces adequate to their needs is at best uncertain, the alternative—a gradual change in their political orientation—is a long-term possibility that should be frankly faced.

Such a change could portend a shift in the balance of power to the distinct advantage of the Soviet Union. America's ability to protect its interests not just in Western Europe—the area where, along with Japan, most is at stake—but in the world might sharply decline. Such dramatic consequences need not necessarily follow a shift in Western Europe's political attitude; but the risk is there. Withdrawals of American troops in significant numbers need not catalyze a shift in the European political attitude; but again the risk is there.

A more immediate danger is that the West's capability for dealing with a wide range of nonsecurity problems would be drastically reduced. At the top of the Atlantic agenda are trade, international monetary arrangements, and aid to developing countries. The danger of splitting apart in dealing with these problems is highlighted by President Nixon's decision on August 15, 1971, to act unilaterally to strengthen the U.S. balance of payments. Suspension of convertibility of the dollar into gold and imposition of a surcharge on imports inevitably create problems for other industrial countries, just as a deteriorating balance of payments had created problems for the United States. A process of recrimination and counter-recrimination could develop. The hoped-for alternative is a series of changes in the international trade and payments system from which all will benefit; but this will depend on close and continuing cooperation among industrial countries. Such cooperation would be harder to achieve if these countries were being driven apart by the kinds of security problems that could follow a substantial unilateral withdrawal of U.S. troops from Europe.

Any study of the issue of force levels implicitly represents an attempt to weigh the risks in reducing them. Those arguing for reductions regard the risks as negligible or as exaggerated by defenders of the status quo, but certainly as acceptable. Those opposing reductions obviously take the other view. Few if any would argue that the current American military posture in Europe should be seen as unchanging or permanent. The conflict arises from differing views of events, of timing, and, to a lesser degree, of priorities.

Chapter 1 sought to explain the assumptions on which the case for a unilateral reduction of European-based American forces is built: (1) an improved and improving East-West political environment, that is, a decline in the threat of outright Soviet attack on or intimidation of

Western Europe; (2) a declining military need for U.S. forces at present levels; (3) a growing European capability to shoulder a substantially larger part of the security burden; and (4) a declining U.S. ability to meet the budgetary and foreign exchange costs of forces in the European theater while also applying adequate resources to domestic problems. How should these considerations be viewed in the light of the preceding chapters?

The East-West Political Environment

Many if not most opponents of existing U.S. NATO commitments are at least partly moved by a sense of deep change in the East-West environment in Europe—a change to which they believe our NATO posture is unresponsive. The period is one of transition; many of the stereotypes of orthodox thinking are up for review. Although Europe remains a source of tension and instability, it is also true that U.S. relations with both halves of Europe are more relaxed—closer to normal— than has been the case. The adversary aspect of relations with de Gaulle's France has been largely effaced. West Germany is relying less on guidance from Washington in its dealings with Moscow. Contacts between Western and Eastern Europe are steadily widening. And our own conflict with Moscow over non-European issues such as Vietnam and the Middle East is seemingly contained by tacit agreement to keep these differences within certain limits. Moreover, both great powers are reluctant to take steps in Europe, as elsewhere, that might unhinge their joint efforts in SALT to maintain stable deterrence.

Still, it is also true that the central assumptions regarding the East-West political environment on which European security arrangements are based remain relevant. If we are in an era of negotiation, the time of confrontation is far from ended. Some progress has been achieved, but its pace and ultimate direction are still unclear. An interim agreement on Berlin and agreements on German-Soviet and German-Polish relations have been attained; but difficult negotiations on other issues, possibly including mutual troop withdrawals, still lie ahead.

Détente and negotiation are obviously desirable and clearly preferable to the harsh and dangerous uncertainties of cold war. But achieving a stable political environment in Europe will be a long, hard business. An important question that will affect the outcome is whether Moscow can, in effect, have it both ways: Can it escape the conflict in a policy that seeks to expand contacts with Western Europe in order to strengthen the Soviet economy and improve the Soviet political position vis-à-vis the West, while maintaining control of Eastern European client states, which then must also be allowed to expand their access to Western European commerce and technology?

The goal for NATO countries should be to turn the duality of Soviet policy to advantage. Little if anything can be done directly to influence Soviet policy toward Eastern Europe. As in the past, however, the thrust of Soviet policy westward can be blunted not only by patient negotiation but also by the continued willingness of NATO member countries, not least the United States, to maintain the integrity of their security system. Anything less will sharpen the temptation before Moscow to seek the best of both worlds. The hope must be that a Soviet failure to exploit Western vulnerabilities will, in time, move Moscow's policy toward greater acceptance of an independent Western Europe immune to political penetration. In turn, the more stable environment implicit in such an evolution might gradually induce a more permissive set of relationships between Moscow and the states of Eastern Europe.

The chief source of instability in the years ahead is likely to be tension arising from Soviet efforts to accommodate polycentric tendencies in Eastern Europe without yielding control. The immediate consequences of these instabilities cannot be predicted, but the possibility of periodic violence that might spread beyond Eastern Europe cannot be ruled out. Again, the problem argues for a Western security system capable of minimizing or containing the consequences of instability in the East, or at least of reducing the possibility of Western European involvement and a wider confrontation.

The operative question is whether and how a unilateral reduction of U.S. forces in Europe would affect a political environment which, although changing, remains bipolar, at least in its security aspect. More precisely, it is a question whether such a step would be matched by a subsequent withdrawal of some Soviet troops from Eastern Europe and improved prospects for negotiations now under way and others likely to follow.

Such questions generate estimates, not answers. In the first instance, at least, a unilateral American troop reduction would probably be seen in Moscow as an opportunity to acquire fresh political leverage in Western Europe, first and foremost in West Germany. The Bonn government's anxiety about the political effects of American withdrawals cannot be seriously questioned. Some would argue that the Germans dramatize the issue; that, viewed objectively, a partial withdrawal of forces should not stimulate a decline of European confidence in U.S. commitments. The difficulty is that the issue resists detachment and objectivity. It is not a question of defense per se, but rather of the Western European perception of political and military requirements underlying security. As Chapter 2 suggests, the point is that a weakening of Bonn's confidence in Washington would almost certainly follow, and would probably stimulate greater Soviet pressure on West Germany.

For these and other reasons it is doubtful, though not to be excluded, that a U.S. reduction would be followed by partial Soviet troop withdrawals from Eastern Europe. Not only would Moscow lack a strong incentive to follow Washington's example, but it might sense an opportunity—possibly also a need—to apply the kind of pressure against West Germany and perhaps other countries that would, in turn, discourage any cut in nearby Soviet military strength. A rising sense of insecurity in West Germany could offer the *opportunity* for intimidation. The *need* might be created by a decision in Bonn to hedge against the uncertainties of a smaller American presence by pressing for close Western European defense cooperation, which might be discouraged only by stern Soviet diplomacy backed by undiminished military strength. As was noted earlier, Soviet forces are deployed in Eastern and Central Europe for multiple purposes; besides meeting an internal bloc security requirement and balancing NATO forces to the West, they remind Western Europe that the Soviet Union, though a global power, is first of all a European power, unlike the United States.

Much the same considerations have tended to dim—at least until recently—the prospects for mutual and balanced force reductions (MBFR). A unilateral U.S. troop reduction would almost certainly discourage mutual cutbacks; Moscow would be reluctant to pay for U.S. withdrawals that seemed likely to be forthcoming in any event. Even if Washington refused to withdraw forces unilaterally, however, there is no assurance that Soviet leaders would agree to mutual reductions. Talks on MBFR will depend on a number of variables—including the degree of risk Soviet leaders are willing to run in Eastern Europe in order to gain potentially rich political dividends in the West; how anxious they are to secure the financial and manpower saving involved; and whether steady reinforcement of the Soviet border with China argues for shifting some forces out of Central Europe.

The question could be a close one for Moscow decision makers. They may decide that pressures in Eastern Europe for a "shakeout" of the political status quo are such that a large mutual reduction (say 30 percent) would represent too large a gamble, but that modest mutual cuts (perhaps on the order of 10 percent) would not affect their hold in the East; the Czech experience showed that Soviet forces can be swiftly and effectively deployed to an unstable zone. For Moscow to bend toward modest cuts would probably be a function of its efforts to loosen West Germany's ties with the West and, specifically, to discourage prospects for a closely organized Western European political community. This Soviet purpose is a reminder that the attitudes of both great powers—toward each other and toward their allies—are to a large degree conditioned by the German problem and latent German bargaining power.

What seems clear is that talks on MBFR will go forward and that they will cover a wide range of issues and consume a great deal of time and energy. MBFR, like SALT, might become a continuing negotiation. And quite possibly a reduction within the 10 percent range will be achieved, depending not only on the factors adduced above but also on Moscow's estimate of whether the United States will make unilateral cuts.

In sum, the East-West political environment, though slowly moderating, remains relatively unstable. If Soviet policy seeks agreement on some issues, such as Berlin, it also dictates efforts to divide the United States from its European allies. In nudging along its détente/negotiation enterprise, Moscow takes one line with Europeans, another with Washington.

This combination of venturesome Soviet diplomacy and undiminished tension in Eastern Europe may prove dangerous for a continent with a long history of violence. Basic instabilities and pressures for change in Eastern Europe, the division of Germany, and tension in Russia and the Balkans lie just beneath the surface and are still capable of generating an accidental emergency or spontaneous outbreak. In that light, the military stability provided by NATO may serve to neutralize political instabilities. One cannot be certain that this is so—nothing in this area is so clear—but the assumption does not seem unreasonable. The Western alliance has withstood strong pressure, notably during Berlin crises, designed to test the strength of the U.S. commitment or to achieve a shift in the balance of power. In a bipolar environment, further challenges to the existing power balance cannot be excluded.

History, in short, does not reveal its alternatives. NATO's contribution in the present East-West environment recalls an eighteenth century London judgment of Robert Walpole—that the tribute to his long rule (marked chiefly by efforts to prevent war) was supplied by the ten years of blundering that came after it.

The Military Balance

American troops in Europe serve two purposes: Together with other NATO forces, they could contain the most likely forms of nonnuclear conflict, at least for a period; and they make more plausible the risk that any large-scale conflict in Europe would involve the use of U.S. nuclear weapons. The argument that considerably fewer troops would serve to contain nonnuclear conflict is hard to sustain, given the commonly accepted estimates of Soviet strength. The argument that considerably fewer uniformed hostages would do as well in underlining the risk of nuclear conflict ignores an essential aspect of that risk: its ambiguity. The other side cannot be certain whether or in what circumstances U.S. nuclear weapons would be used. But common sense suggests that their use would be more likely after considerable nonnuclear fighting had occurred. The nuclear option can thus be seen as one that might conceivably be chosen, but *only* after both sides had taken full account of whatever fighting had occurred. In this sense, a credible nuclear option requires a relatively high nuclear threshold— that is, deployment of forces adequate to provide the necessary period of nonnuclear combat during which every alternative to the use of nuclear weapons could be methodically explored and exhausted.

Deterrence rests on allied confidence in, as well as Soviet attitudes toward, NATO strategy. This strategy now relies on centralized U.S. control of nuclear weapons in Europe at all stages of an emergency or hostilities. Allied countries, no less than the USSR, know that the United States would be most unlikely to exercise the nuclear option until after nonnuclear combat had reached a high threshold. Among the perceived effects of a substantial withdrawal of U.S. forces from Europe would be a lowering of that threshold; European confidence in American commitments would almost certainly decline sharply.

In addition to the issues of deterrence and allied confidence, three questions regarding U.S. military strength in Europe are of direct concern:

Are the forces of NATO and the Warsaw Pact in balance? Although no two experts fully agree on the exact military balance in Europe, many perceive a crude balance between NATO and Warsaw Pact ground and air forces. Chapter 3 suggests that the current advantage of the Warsaw Pact in forces readily available in Central Europe is partially offset by other factors that favor the West. In other words, though there may not be a balance in the narrowest military sense, there probably *is* a balance in the political-military context of deterrence.

Do American forces in Europe meet plausible military needs? Judgments of the military balance must be partly subjective; beyond a certain point, the data base is mocked by innumerable unknowns, asymmetries, and imponderables. What is clear, however, is that a rough military balance is essential to the stability of deterrence and that American contributions are essential to that balance. Quantitatively, U.S. forces constitute about one-fourth of NATO strength on the central front. Qualitatively, however, American units would be hard to replace; neither the Russians nor the Europeans would expect European units to make the same contribution to deterrence. Moreover, as was noted in Chapter 4, it is improbable that departing American units would be replaced at all. Given the crucial military role of the Seventh Army and the preponderantly American contribution of air defense and air superiority in southern Germany, significant reductions of these U.S. forces could create serious gaps on the central front and degrade a strategy based on forward defense.

If and when U.S. forces are reduced, which of them should be cut first? Chapter 3 suggests that (1) ideally a U.S. force cut in Europe should not be made entirely at the expense of one service component; (2) in the case of sizable reductions, it would not be desirable to alter significantly the present balance between combat and combat support capabilities; and that (3) if a modest cut on the order of 10 percent were required, the best choice would be a package of across-the-board reductions that would concentrate on the support and back-up area for all three services and affect initial combat potential only marginally. Alternatively, general purpose forces could be reduced without affecting either combat or combat support capabilities on the European central front by eliminating one of two carrier task forces from the Sixth Fleet in the Mediterranean and another from the Atlantic fleet. If and as the Middle East situation becomes less unstable, such reductions might become feasible, especially if the Navy could improve its "surge" capability—the time required to send another carrier to the area in time of emergency.

Conceivably the Sixth Fleet, which has considerably greater power than the Soviet Mediterranean fleet, could be restructured and modernized in a way that would permit economies while not doing violence to its political role beyond Europe. However, this political role is unlikely to become any less critical; indeed, the contrary will probably prove to be the case. Tensions in Southern Europe, and the especially worrisome uncertainties of Yugoslavia's post-Tito political course, may give Washington a strong incentive to avoid any gesture—notably reductions in either U.S. land- or sea-based forces in Europe—that could be misunderstood by the countries directly concerned.

More substantial cuts in U.S. forces would probably dictate radical change and restructuring of NATO forces on the central front. With such restructuring, German territorial and other fixed defense forces would hold a forward line, while largely armored and mobile allied forces were positioned behind this line to counter any Soviet breakthrough. It is doubtful, however, that such a step could be taken without arousing large political uncertainties—on both the allied and Soviet sides—that could seriously degrade deterrence.

Western Europe's Capabilities

Ideally, the Western alliance should be configured by two groups—North America and Western Europe—not only about equal in size and defending the same civilization, but with roughly equivalent responsibilities. Instead, reality imposes the unequal division of responsibility inherent in a security relationship between a superpower and a group of small and medium powers, no one of which is able to defend itself alone or assume a significantly larger share of the joint burden. Washington and the European NATO governments have often and long disagreed on strategic questions; but the general proposition that Western Europe can be defended only so long as the United States maintains not only its commitments but a strong continental military presence is close to being an article of faith in European political and defense circles.

This continued dependence on the United States might appear to be an incentive for Europeans to do more in their own defense. But for governments influenced by other considerations—not the least of which are domestic political limits on their capabilities—it is an incentive to maintain the status quo and to avoid the internal difficulties that would be provoked by efforts to increase defense spending. Other factors also play a role. The growing indifference to defense and security in Western Europe is partly traceable to reduced tensions and expanding East-West contacts, even as technology and inflation drive up the cost of defense. So long as Western European governments see their defense programs in essentially national terms, so long will they question the usefulness of significantly increasing their programs.

If it is true that America bears a disproportionate share of the NATO burden, it is also true (as Chapter 5 suggests) that the disparity in military effort between the United States and Europe, though still large, is measurably narrowing. But mere figures are misleading. Much of the nearly $25 billion that Western European countries, including France, spend annually on defense represents duplication. An agreement to eliminate a large part of this duplication by rationalizing European defense spending, such as might follow progress toward European unity, would mean that the same investment would return considerably more defense. And the greater identity of political view—the sense of unity—implicit in joint defense arrangements, whether modest or sweeping, would represent a less tangible but incomparably greater source of security.

A strong Western Europe, endowed with a sense of identity and coherence, would be less vulnerable to intimidation or to other destabilizing influences (some of them internal). As was noted earlier, the existence of such a Western Europe could also help to moderate the political environment by encouraging progress, however gradual, toward Soviet acceptance of the Western security system as a fact of life and by helping to create a climate in which more permissive relations between Russia and Eastern European societies might slowly develop (even though the immediate consequence of major moves toward Western European unity might be a tightening of the Soviet grip on its empire).

Europe in the 1970s is unlikely, however, to conform to any of the models or designs of even the most farsighted planners and statesmen. Nothing so clear cut as, say, a federation of Western European states is likely to emerge for a long time, if it ever does. Nor, on the other hand, are Europeans likely to bury the impulse toward unity. This mixed prospect argues for maintaining the present U.S. force levels in the short and middle term, even as it holds out some hope of eventually reducing them. For a crucial function of the U.S. defense guarantees and military presence is to help sustain Western Europe's episodic course toward cohesion and closer organization.

Some have argued that a decision by the United States to reduce its military presence would stimulate the European unity movement as nothing else could. Perhaps. It is at least as likely, however, that some Western European countries would react by seeking détente and accommodation, not from a position of relative strength as at present, but at the expense of Western security arrangements. Nor is it easy to imagine the major Western European countries—Britain, France, and West Germany—moving boldly and together toward regional unity against a background of declining confidence in American security guarantees. This is a possibility, but no more than that. The other possibility—that these countries would pursue more independent and divisive policies—is at least as strong.

In short, collective security arrangements are essential both to the European unity movement and to genuine and lasting détente. These two large purposes are, in fact, closely related. So uniquely difficult an enterprise as the unity movement requires a stable political environment. Whether it could survive the additional complication of Soviet opposition—possibly even intimidation—against a Western Europe increasingly doubtful of its security seems at least questionable. Nor, for reasons already noted, can the pursuit of détente be safely divorced from reliable security arrangements: Any durable East-West political accommodation will require a stable military as well as political environment.

Governments have the problem of reordering long-familiar relationships at a time when the continuity of political and strategic requirements tends to be obscured, but not significantly altered, by marked changes in political and cultural attitudes. How, for example, can the NATO system be rebalanced to correct the excessive dependence of Western Europeans on America before the strains of this one-sided relationship enfeeble the structure? Chapter 4 suggests that rebalancing the system will require a new political dynamic that could probably be supplied only by a Western Europe moving in stages toward some reasonably advanced degree of unity.

Although Washington can do little directly to affect European political development in the short term, American policy and attitudes will greatly influence Western Europe's preferences over the longer term. This means making clear continuing U.S. support for Western European unity and a willingness to accept the diminished U.S. role that progress in that direction would impose. Failing such progress, the alliance system must bear the burden not only of its structural anomaly, but of the differences and divergences between the United States and Western Europe that have accumulated with time. Some would ask whether the Atlantic system can realistically be expected to survive these difficulties, or whether Washington should seek an alternative. The answer is that no better or more reliable alternative is now visible, whether in terms of American or European interests. A reduction in U.S. forces would be unlikely to lead to increased European effort. Current arrangements allow the United States to defend its interests at the point of greatest danger and potential instability. That is the heart of the issue.

The Financial Issue

How large and disproportionate a financial burden do our troops in Europe represent? Can we in fact save money by bringing back forces from Europe? If not, in what circumstances are savings possible? The answers to these questions are frequently assumed rather than derived from systematic analysis. The danger is that we might seek changes in force levels for the wrong reasons and in ways that could ultimately cost money rather than save it.

It is scarcely surprising that the forces we maintain for European contingencies—whether stationed in Europe or in the United States—represent half the total U.S. conventional forces. Preparing for military contingencies in Europe and providing forces that might discourage their occurrence have been a primary U.S. security interest for almost three decades. Indeed, even if NATO disappeared, some or all of these forces would still be required, though none might be positioned in Europe. Furthermore, in an emergency they are available for contingencies outside Europe. Thus the estimated annual cost of these forces in no sense represents an *incremental* cost for the United States arising from NATO.

What of the U.S. forces actually stationed in Europe? Chapter 5 points out that they represent less than half of the total U.S. forces earmarked for European contingencies. We would not save money simply by bringing them back and stationing them in the United States; they would cost about as much to maintain in this country as in Europe, and we would have to build additional transport capability to send them to Europe in an emergency.

Saving money would be possible only if we reduced the forces we maintain for European contingencies, wherever those forces are stationed. Such a reduction would be likely, however, only after we had virtually eliminated the sizable peacetime forces we now maintain for Asian contingencies, since Europe represents the first priority claim on general purpose forces. Put another way, a cut in forces earmarked for NATO would imply a very large reduction in the total U.S. peacetime force structure and a return to a strategy of heavy reliance on nuclear deterrence. Furthermore, should we decide to cut forces for Europe, we might prefer, on both military and cost grounds, to deactivate units stationed here rather than in Europe.

In short, the budgetary cost question should be viewed in terms of how U.S. forces for NATO fit into the peacetime general purpose force structure and the cost-cutting priorities that emerge from this relationship. These priorities strongly indicate that under almost any conceivable force structure alternatives, cutting U.S. division strength in Europe would not be likely to produce budget savings and could, in the end, be more costly.

None of this is to suggest that economies could not be made by eliminating redundant capabilities or outdated U.S. military functions in Europe. Over the past five years, U.S. military strength in Europe has been cut by more than 30,000 men through such efficiency measures. Doubtless further reductions through adjustment and streamlining are still possible and should be pursued.

Foreign exchange costs arising from U.S. forces in Europe raise a different set of issues. The smaller part is a question of cost sharing: Who should bear the operating cost of local facilities in Europe where American troops are stationed? But the bulk of the NATO foreign exchange issue relates not to who bears the resource or real cost of collective defense but to how the international monetary system can most effectively operate.

NATO responsibilities now cost the U.S. almost $2 billion a year in foreign exchange. Withdrawal of our forces from Europe, however, would not produce anything like a corresponding improvement in our balance of payments. The balance-of-payments consequences of current foreign exchange outlays have been mitigated by special German purchases of U.S. military equipment, by German cooperation in holding a large portion of German international reserves in dollars, and more recently by German revaluations of the deutsche mark. Nevertheless, existing arrangements have not been satisfactory. It should be possible to negotiate cost-sharing arrangements and improved ground rules to neutralize NATO-induced foreign exchange flows and thereby to insulate decisions on NATO forces from the balance-of-payments consequences—the more so if the international payments system is improved in the negotiations to follow President Nixon's suspension of the dollar's convertibility into gold.

More generally, Chapter 5 argues that the United States should negotiate cost-sharing and foreign exchange arrangements with European NATO countries that would enable Washington to view its forces in Europe as having financial effects no different from those of troops stationed at home. The end result, while removing foreign exchange concerns from the debate, would bring only a modest increase in defense costs for Western Europe; by the same token it would not appreciably diminish the total budgetary cost to the United States of

the forces it maintains for the defense of Europe. NATO would benefit if the negotiations served to clarify on both sides of the Atlantic the
financial facts underlying the question of what forces the United States
should maintain for European contingencies. For Washington, the incremental cost of these forces—that is, the amount in excess of what
we would spend for them if NATO did not exist—is relatively small;
for Europe, the total cost of these forces is about equal to what all European NATO member countries together spend on defense; for
both, decisions about the modest amounts at issue between the United
States and Western Europe could have a disproportionate effect on
collective defense, for better or for worse.

The Conditions for Change

The chapters summarized above suggest a continuing need for the
present number of U.S. forces in Europe and outline steps to share
their costs more evenly. These steps in turn could emphasize the per-
manence of NATO security arrangements in ways that might improve prospects for the kinds of change—in both the East-West environment and in Western Europe—that could eventually permit a
reduction in U.S. force levels. Thus the question is not whether, but
when and how, such a reduction will take place. This study argues that
the *when* awaits basic political changes and that the *how* will emerge
from multilateral decision-making. Admittedly, this is a counsel of
patience—a rare quality that is especially elusive today.

For the issue of costs is only one aspect of the larger question of
priorities and allocation of resources that currently preoccupies most
Western countries. Governments are being buffeted by forces they
may not fully comprehend, but which exert increasing influence. Stu-
dents and others reject the values of a high-consumption society or,
perhaps more accurately, what they regard as the absence of values in
such a society. Other more tangible and more pressing problems—en-
vironmental pollution, the pressures of rapidly evolving technology,
the intractability of poverty—pose valid and growing claims on na-

tional attention. In its absorption with these emerging issues, society may ignore others that, partly because they are more familiar and have been with us longer, appear anachronistic to some and incomprehensible to others.

In this period of collective mea culpa, society tends to react with growing vigor to its domestic problems and with declining will to the no less hard and unyielding tasks of promoting a stable world order. How governments deal with the latter may influence the lives of this and succeeding generations as much as how they deal with the more dramatic and immediate social problems that were too long ignored and that clearly do threaten an acceptable way of life on the planet. To stress one challenge to our civilization at the expense of another risks compromising the future.

Somewhat paradoxically, European security still depends on the balance between American and Soviet forces concentrated on either side of the Elbe. One day Western and Eastern Europe may be able to assume primary responsibility for their own destinies, but Western Europe now lacks the will and Eastern Europe the means to effect such a transition. The European system is distorted by the very primacy of the great powers, whose unique burdens give them a vested interest in the stability offered by the status quo, whatever its vexations. This point cannot be pushed too far. The Soviet Union, on balance, would undoubtedly be pleased to see NATO break up and the American forces withdraw, destabilizing though this might be. Washington, in turn, would be pleased to see Western Europe achieve the kind of unity that would allow a redistribution of the defense burden. But the system finds its virtue in the absence of any likely or mutually acceptable alternative. Moscow prefers the status quo to any visible substitute, a political reality that has discouraged flexibility or innovation on the Western side.

Any acceptable major revision of the status quo will require movement toward both closer organization in Western Europe and détente at several levels throughout Europe, combined with a limited but clearly perceived identity of interest between the United States and the Soviet Union in moving toward accommodation—toward an acknowledgment of their joint responsibility to confine beneath a certain level of violence any conflict in which they might be involved, to set limits on the arms race, to reduce their military confrontation in Europe, and to lessen the risk of hostilities, especially in Europe. The superpowers are in the first stages of learning to bargain and reach agreement on these shared problems. They have reached an agreement on Berlin, are negotiating in SALT, and look toward negotiation on mutual troop withdrawals in Europe. If and as all these efforts bear fruit, the present system of European security may gradually become anachronistic, if not irrelevant, in all eyes. Certainly the determination of all Europeans to play a larger role in matters affecting their security will grow; and we can hope that *both* of the great powers will develop a corresponding impatience with an unliquidated burden dating almost to the last war. But that is looking far ahead, perhaps beyond the 1970s.

For Western governments, then, it becomes a question of pursuing East-West negotiations and supporting steps that could strengthen and perhaps help to rebalance the Western alliance, while not allowing internal stresses to efface the special, hence fragile quality of inter-Atlantic relationships. These relationships will be subject to shock—as the events of August 15, 1971 in the area of international monetary policy so graphically demonstrated.

Without losing hope or pursuing chimerical alternatives, Western governments must recognize that rarely do events and the political choices before them lead to entirely rational or ideal resolutions of great issues. Eventual change is likely, but for a good many years the system for defending Western Europe is unlikely to bend either to the logic of a twin-pillar inter-Atlantic system emerging from a united Western Europe capable of unitary political decision, or to mutual force withdrawals by the United States and the Soviet Union so broad as to reduce substantially the great-power military confrontation in Central Europe. Instead, something less symmetrical though no less viable is likely to persist. However anomalous, this system has kept the peace in Europe for more than two decades. It is likely to remain the safest, least troublesome, and quite possibly the most economical way to meet the security requirements of NATO countries and at the same time to provide a basis for healthy change.

Notes

Chapter 1

1. *Congressional Record*, daily ed., Jan. 24, 1970, p. S496.
2. Ibid.
3. *The North Atlantic Treaty, Pt. 1: Administration Witnesses*, Hearings before the Senate Committee on Foreign Relations, 81 Cong. 1 sess. (1949), Pt. 1, p. 47.
4. Ibid., p. 308.
5. Ibid., p. 309.
6. *Congressional Record*, daily ed., May 18, 1971, p. S7217.
7. James A. Johnson, "The New Generation of Isolationists," *Foreign Affairs*, Vol. 49 (October 1970), pp. 139–40.
8. *Congressional Record*, daily ed., Jan. 24, 1970, pp. S493–95.
9. Ibid., p. S496.
10. Ibid., p. S493.
11. Ibid.
12. *Congressional Record*, daily ed., May 19, 1971, p. S7427.
13. *Congressional Record*, Vol. 112, Pt. 16, 89 Cong. 2 sess. (1966), p. 21829.
14. Stuart Symington, "In Search for Sound Foreign Policy" (speech in Kansas City, Missouri, May 19, 1969; press release).
15. Alain C. Enthoven and K. Wayne Smith, "What Forces for NATO? And From Whom?" *Foreign Affairs*, Vol. 48 (October 1969), p. 90.
16. *New York Times*, Dec. 3, 1970.
17. *Congressional Record*, Vol. 112, Pt. 16, 89 Cong. 2 sess. (1966), p. 21829.
18. *Congressional Record*, daily ed., Jan. 24, 1970, p. S493.
19. *Congressional Record*, daily ed., May 18, 1971, pp. S7215–16.
20. Charles H. Percy, "Paying for NATO," *Washington Monthly*, Vol. 2 (July 1970), p. 32.
21. Ibid.
22. J. Robert Schaetzel, speech delivered to the German Foreign Policy Association, Bonn, West Germany, Feb. 12, 1970.
23. *U.S. Security Agreements and Commitments Abroad, Pt. 10: United States Forces in*

Europe, Hearings before the Subcommittee on U.S. Security Agreements and Commitments Abroad of the Senate Committee on Foreign Relations, 91 Cong. 2 sess. (1970), Vol. 2, Pt. 10, p. 2085.

24. *Congressional Record*, daily ed., April 20, 1970, pp. S5957–58.

25. *Congressional Record*, daily ed., May 24, 1970, pp. S495–96. The decision by the German government in May 1971 to float the mark increased the cost of U.S. forces based in Germany by another 3 to 4 percent and could also lead to another revaluation.

26. *Congressional Record*, daily ed., May 19, 1971, p. S7395.

27. *U.S. Security Agreements and Commitments Abroad, Pt. 10: United States Forces in Europe*, Hearings, p. 2248.

28. Enthoven and Smith, "What Forces for NATO?" p. 82.

29. Carl Kaysen, "Military Strategy, Military Forces and Arms Control," in Kermit Gordon (ed.), *Agenda for the Nation* (Brookings Institution, 1968), p. 572.

30. *Congressional Record*, Vol. 115, Pt. 10, 91 Cong. 1 sess. (1969), p. 13055.

31. *U.S. Security Agreements and Commitments Abroad, Pt. 10: United States Forces in Europe*, Hearings, p. 2240.

32. *Congressional Record*, daily ed., May 19, 1971, p. S7426.

Chapter 2

1. *Congressional Record*, daily ed., Jan. 24, 1970, p. S496.

2. See, for example, David Calleo, *The Atlantic Fantasy: The U.S., NATO, and Europe* (Johns Hopkins Press, 1970). According to Calleo, "Czechoslovakia did not renew the Cold War. While their reaction to the Czech crisis suggests that some people in the West would almost seem to welcome another harsh era of confrontation, they are not likely to have their wish. Today's Russians are far too conciliatory. In spite of the Czech intervention, itself undertaken with considerable hesitation and restraint, Russia obviously desired a continuing European détente and had no wish to provoke a new Cold War." (p. 82) Calleo advocates shifting the defense burden (including nuclear weapons) to a European nucleus, something the Soviets purport to dislike even more than they do the present "Atlanticist" system.

3. Compare the remarks of Henry A. Kissinger, "Central Issues of American Foreign Policy," in Kermit Gordon (ed.), *Agenda for the Nation* (Brookings Institution, 1968), p. 609. Kissinger also notes that the attempt to gauge Soviet purposes and intentions leads to the additional confusion of deflecting us from articulating American purposes, whatever Soviet intentions.

4. As Foreign Minister Gromyko put it in 1969, "European affairs occupy a large and important place in the foreign policy of the Soviet Union. Many highly important threads in world politics as a whole extend from Europe and toward Europe. Our country's fate has frequently hinged on the development of events in Europe." *Pravda*, July 11, 1969.

5. See, for example, L. Bezymensky, "A Pan-European Task," *New Times*, July 3, 1970, p. 3, where the writer depicts Europe as being in a state of "metastability"—"the state in which the least disturbance will start off a furious reaction."

6. For a rather explicit Soviet analysis along these lines, see E. Novoseltsev, "Europe Twenty-Five Years Later," *International Affairs* (Moscow, July 1970), pp. 15–22.

7. N. Yuryev, "European Security: A Dictate of Our Times," *International Affairs* (Moscow, August 1970), p. 3.

8. For a salient analysis, together with broad policy recommendations, see Zbigniew Brzezinski, "America and Europe," *Foreign Affairs*, Vol. 49 (October 1970), pp. 11–30.

9. For a more detailed analysis, see Richard Lowenthal, "The Sparrow in the Cage," *Problems of Communism*, Vol. 17 (November–December 1968), pp. 2–28, especially pp. 5–6.

10. *Pravda*, July 11, 1969.

11. V. Matveyev, "Lessons of History and European Security," *International Affairs* (Moscow, June 1970), p. 13. Italics in original.

12. Novoseltsev, ibid., p. 21.

13. Responding to a speech by the U.S. permanent representative to NATO advancing such a proposal, a Soviet commentator deemed it "provocative" and "the limit." *Pravda*, June 14, 1970.

14. Novoseltsev, ibid., p. 22.

15. Compare the emphasis accorded by Soviet commentators to the nominal (and apparently minuscule) Romanian participation in the autumn 1970 exercises; *New York Times*, Oct. 15, 1970.

16. Compare the text of the Budapest memorandum in *Pravda*, June 27, 1970.

17. *New York Times*, May 5, 1971.

18. Compare the text of a roundtable discussion on European security, especially the remarks by Radio Moscow foreign affairs commentator V. Kudryavtsev. Moscow Domestic Service in Russian, 0900 GMT, Aug. 23, 1970.

19. A. Vetrov, "Economic Ties between Socialist and Capitalist States," *International Affairs* (Moscow, September 1970), pp. 10–11.

20. Ibid., p. 11.

21. V. Shishkov, "All-European Cooperation: Economic Aspects," *New Times*, Aug. 19, 1970, p. 25.

22. Y. Zhukov in *Pravda*, July 23, 1970. This article is part of a series by this commentator on U.S. economic hegemony over Western Europe.

23. Shiskov, ibid., p. 24.

24. D. Melnikov, *Literaturnaya Gazeta*, Sept. 2, 1970. References to the grandeur of France have been legion. For an account of some extraordinary flattery of Germany, see "Europäische Visionen eines sowjetischen Gastes," *Frankfurter Allgemeine Zeitung*, Sept. 24, 1970.

25. Zbigniew Brzezinski, *Alternative to Partition: For a Broader Conception of America's Role in Europe* (McGraw-Hill, 1965), pp. 79–80.

26. TASS International Service in English, 0551 GMT, June 29, 1970.

27. *Pravda*, Aug. 25, 1970.

28. *Pravda*, July 29, 1970.

29. L. Yugov, "Italy's European Problems," *International Affairs* (Moscow, August 1970), p. 49.

30. For a perceptive Western analysis that did see precisely this possibility, see Pierre Hassner, "Change and Security in Europe. Part I: The Background," *Adelphi Papers*, No. 45, February 1968, p. 20.

31. Compare, for example, the editorials "European Horizons," *New Times*, No. 34, Aug. 26, 1970, and "Next Step: Translating Possibilities into Reality," ibid., Sept. 16, 1970; *Krasnaya zvezda*, Aug. 14 and Sept. 8, 1970; and the remarks of Y. Zhukov in West Germany, *Die Zeit* (North American edition), Oct. 6, 1970.

32. Compare Podgorny's remarks at the official reception for Pompidou, *Pravda*, Oct. 7, 1970.

33. Yugov, ibid., p. 50.

34. Suslov, speech on the 53rd anniversary of the revolution, and commentary of M. Kobrin as reported on Radio Moscow, 0230 GMT, Nov. 9, 1970.

35. S. I. Beglov, "The United States and Western Europe: Some Aspects of Their Mutual Relations," *SShA* [USA] (June 1970), pp. 3–13.

36. Novoseltsev, ibid., p. 22. Compare the citation by *Pravda*, Sept. 26, 1969, of Romain Rolland: "A Pan-Europe without Russia is absurd. Against Russia it is villainy."

37. TASS International Service in English, 0630 GMT, June 26, 1970.

38. Moscow Domestic Service in Russian, 1900 GMT, Oct. 4, 1970.

39. Novoseltsev, ibid., p. 21; Matveyev, ibid., p. 12.

40. Beglov, ibid.

41. Ibid.

42. Compare the extensive and balanced discussion of the pros and cons in Thomas W. Wolfe, *Soviet Power and Europe, 1945–1970* (Johns Hopkins Press, 1970), pp. 499–515, and the same writer's "Soviet Approaches to SALT," *Problems of Communism*, Vol. 19, (September–October 1970), pp. 1–10.

43. Helmut Schmidt, "Germany in the Era of Negotiations," *Foreign Affairs*, Vol. 49 (October 1970), p. 41. See also Kurt Becker, "Amerika erhöht den Preis," *Die Zeit* (North American edition), Oct. 13, 1970.

44. Hassner, ibid., p. 24.

Chapter 3

1. This refers primarily to active defenses, although the USSR's investment in rudimentary ABMs suggests that it gives a higher priority to air and missile defenses than does the United States. On civil defense (population protection as well as evacuation and survival training), the USSR currently spends between five and ten times as much as the United States—depending on how one resolves the difficult question of what to count. See Leon Goure, "Soviet Civil Defense Revisited 1966–1969," RAND Memorandum 6113-PR (The RAND Corporation, 1969; processed).

2. For press reports on Helsinki II, see William Beecher, *New York Times*, Oct. 20, 1970, and Chalmers Roberts and Henry Owen, *Washington Post*, Nov. 3 and 5, 1970, respectively. For the administration's view on SALT, see the President's Feb. 25, 1971 message to Congress, *United States Foreign Policy for the 1970's: Building for Peace*, pp. 146–52.

3. According to the Institute for Strategic Studies (see *The Military Balance, 1970–71*, p. 105, and *Strategic Survey, 1969*, p. 27, both published in London, 1970), the United States had an intercontinental delivery force of 1,000 Minutemen, 656 Polaris missiles, and 540 long-range bombers; this is in rough parity with a Soviet offensive strategic force of 1,300 to 1,500 intercontinental ballistic missiles (ICBMs), 230 submarine-launched missiles, and 150 long-range bombers. Both nations have or are acquiring multiple warheads for their missiles, but the United States appears to have a qualitative edge with MIRV. On the other hand, the Soviet Union allocates more men and aircraft to strategic defense—including air defense missiles—than does the United States. And while Russia is thought to have a quantitative lead in ABMs with its Galosh missile, the American Safeguard ABM system is expected to be superior in qualitative terms. An analysis in the *New York*

Times (Dec. 20, 1970) estimates that the United States will have a 1975 "throwable warhead" inventory of 7,494. Soviet ICBMs are given as 300 SS-9s (MIRV-capable) and 800 SS-11s plus various of the older SS-7s, and SS-8s and some solid-fuel SS-13 rockets. The Soviet warhead total may be smaller than America's but the total megatonnage larger. The most recent figure for Soviet ICBMs (1,440) is contained in Table 2 of Secretary Laird's Statement on the 1972 Defense Budget before the House Armed Services Committee, March 9, 1971.

4. That U.S. forces in Europe relate to the cold war and not to World War II is shown by the fact that the wartime level of some 3 million men reached a low of 100,000 in Germany by 1947. A single division was formed out of the occupation constabulary in response to the Berlin blockade. After the initial buildup of American forces during the Korean war, the number in Germany (there were more in Europe as a whole) remained more or less constant at 240,000 to 250,000 during the 1950s—the period of "massive retaliation." It rose again during the Berlin crisis of 1961–62 but gradually declined to just over 200,000 during the "flexible response" period of the middle and late sixties. See Horst Menderhausen, "Troop Stationing in Germany: Value and Cost," RAND Memorandum 5881-PR (The RAND Corporation, 1968; processed), p. 8; James D. Hessman, "U.S. Forces in Europe," *Armed Forces Journal*, July 11, 1970, p. 20; and *U.S. Security Agreements and Commitments Abroad, Pt. 10: United States Forces in Europe*, Hearings before the Subcommittee on U.S. Security Agreements and Commitments Abroad of the Senate Committee on Foreign Relations, 91 Cong. 2 sess. (1970), Vol. 2, Pt. 10, p. 2154.

5. *The Transatlantic Bargain* (Harper & Row, 1970), pp. 62–63.

6. William Beecher, *New York Times*, Dec. 4, 1969 and Oct. 28, 1970, and Drew Middleton, *New York Times*, June 9 and 10, 1970.

7. The argument continues between advocates of low-yield "clean" weapons and those who believe that the collateral damage would be unacceptable even from restricted battlefield use. See Sir Solly Zuckerman, "Judgment and Control in Modern Warfare," *Foreign Affairs*, Vol. 40 (January 1962), pp. 196–212. Two authors advocate nuclearizing NATO's defense with modern, discrete warheads: Phillip A. Karber in *Orbis* (Summer 1970) and Edwin F. Black in the American Security Council's *Washington Report*, Dec. 21, 1970. Both articles are reprinted in the *Congressional Record*, daily ed., Dec. 30, 1970, pp. E10880–85.

8. Statement of the Secretary of Defense, *Department of Defense Appropriations for 1964*, Hearings before a Subcommittee of the House Committee on Appropriations, 88 Cong. 1 sess. (1963), p. 101.

9. *The Military Balance, 1970–71* (London: Institute for Strategic Studies, 1970), p. 95.

10. Robert E. Osgood's *NATO: The Entangling Alliance* (University of Chicago Press, 1962) has a good review of the tactical nuclear debates of the 1950s (pp. 102–46).

11. See William W. Kaufmann, *The McNamara Strategy* (Harper & Row, 1964), Chaps. 2 and 3. For a dissenting view, see Bernard Brodie, "What Price Conventional Capabilities in Europe?" *The Reporter*, May 23, 1963.

12. For a current review of Soviet capabilities by the Supreme Allied Commander, Europe, see the interview with General Andrew J. Goodpaster in *U.S. News and World Report*, Dec. 7, 1970, pp. 61–63. A similar analysis by his predecessor, General Lyman L. Lemnitzer, is given in *United States Relations with Europe in the Decade of the 1970's*, Hearings before the Subcommittee on Europe, House Committee on Foreign Affairs, 91 Cong. 2 sess. (1970), pp. 57–63.

13. *United States Relations with Europe*, Hearings, p. 172.

14. The ex post facto justification for the invasion of Czechoslovakia ("defending the interests of world socialism") is outlined in an article by Sergei Kovalyov in *Pravda*, Sept. 26, 1968, translated in *Survival* (London: Institute for Strategic Studies), November 1968, pp. 375–78.

15. See Timothy W. Stanley, "A Strategic Doctrine for NATO in the 1970's," *Orbis*, Spring 1969, pp. 87–99; reprinted as "NATO's Strategic Doctrine," *Survival*, November 1969, pp. 342–49.

16. Quoted from an unpublished manuscript by Thornton Read.

17. Unless otherwise indicated, the source of these data is *The Military Balance, 1970–71*.

18. This estimate includes items not in the formal Soviet defense budget and is based on conversion at estimated purchasing power value; see *The Military Balance, 1970–71*, pp. 10–11, for an explanation of the methodology.

19. These figures are aggregated from the country sections in *The Military Balance, 1970–71*.

20. *Washington Post*, Oct. 30, 1970. These 5,000 tanks, however, were not recently "discovered," as implied in the article. The question has been whether to count those that are not manned and maintained on a "ready" basis or that are older models and sometimes lack spare parts.

21. Memorandum of Oct. 22, 1968 from Assistant Secretary of Defense Alain C. Enthoven appended to the 1968 Report of the Military Committee of the North Atlantic Assembly, Senator John Sherman Cooper, rapporteur. *Congressional Record*, daily ed., Oct. 14, 1970, p. S18013.

22. 1969 Report Presented to the Military Committee of the North Atlantic Assembly, Appendix II. *Congressional Record*, daily ed., Oct. 14, 1970, p. S18023.

23. *Statement of Secretary of Defense Robert S. McNamara before the Senate Armed Services Committee on the Fiscal Year 1969–73 Defense Program and 1969 Defense Budget* (Jan. 22, 1968), p. 80.

24. Information on reinforcement capabilities was furnished to the Senate Foreign Relations Subcommittee on U.S. Security Agreements and Commitments Abroad, but all numbers were deleted from the published record. See *United States Forces in Europe*, Hearings, Pt. 10, p. 2072.

25. *Statement of Secretary of Defense Robert S. McNamara . . . on the . . . 1969 Defense Budget*, p. 81.

26. *The Military Balance, 1970–71*, pp. 7–8 and 92–93. This figure does not include Hungarian forces or those Soviet divisions that might be committed in the Northern European or Baltic area. The manpower estimate is based on the ISS-reported strength of the average Soviet formation (10,000 men) and adds 50 percent of this divisional manpower for nondivisional support and command and control under mobilization conditions. The indirect and logistic support would also be substantial on both sides, but it is not included in these projections in order to be consistent with the ISS data.

27. See the U.S. Defense Department data compiled in Senator Cooper's report to the Military Committee of the North Atlantic Assembly, reprinted in the *Congressional Record*, daily ed., Oct. 14, 1970, pp. S17994 and S18011–13.

28. These figures are derived from the country data given in *The Military Balance, 1970–71*. They assume 1 Canadian division, 5 British divisions, and up to 16 American divisions (the equivalent of 5 now in Europe, 3 in the strategic reserve for NATO, and

1 Marine division, plus 7 division forces from other active and reserve forces). The United States has maintained about 29 Army and Marine division force equivalents, of which 20 have been active. See Appendix D of Secretary Laird's Defense Report to Congress of Feb. 20, 1970, and Charles L. Schultze and others, *Setting National Priorities: The 1971 Budget* (Brookings Institution, 1970), pp. 37–44.

29. This assumes that the Soviet Union could add 40 divisions to its M+30 European force—for a total of 110 divisions by M+90 in Northern and Central Europe—and that East Germany, Poland, and Czechoslovakia could add 7 more for a total of 40 divisions during the same period. This is about the number of units maintained in the higher categories of readiness, according to the ISS. This would leave the Soviet Union with 47 divisions for its southern and Far Eastern fronts and for general reserves, and it would leave the Eastern European countries with 17 uncommitted divisions. It is assumed that paramilitary formations would supplement these for internal security.

30. The manpower estimates are based on the rule of thumb stated in n. 26: that is, adding 50 percent of the division manpower for combat support.

31. Alain C. Enthoven, "Arms and Men: The Military Balance in Europe," *Interplay*, May 1969. Estimates can range from a Pact division equivalent to a conservative 0.9 of a NATO division to an optimistic 0.3 or 0.4, depending on what comparisons are used—manpower, firepower, or equipment—and what weight is given to indirect support. Two-thirds, or 0.67, is a reasonable compromise that most analysts would accept.

32. See President Nixon's message to Congress, *United States Foreign Policy for the 1970s: Building for Peace*, Feb. 25, 1971, pp. 24 and 139–40.

33. Alain C. Enthoven and K. Wayne Smith, "What Forces for NATO? And From Whom?" *Foreign Affairs*, Vol. 48 (October 1969).

34. Lord Wigg, the British Paymaster General, writing in *The Times* (London), Feb. 20, 1969.

35. A special issue of the *NATO Letter*, September 1970, details the annual increase and discusses the significance of Soviet naval activities in the Northeast Atlantic and Mediterranean areas. Another useful reference is *Military Forces and Political Conflicts in the Mediterranean*, a group of papers published by the Atlantic Institute (Paris) as Atlantic Paper 1, January 1970.

36. Drew Middleton, "NATO Is Stressing Its Mobile Force," *New York Times*, Dec. 13, 1970.

37. Timothy W. Stanley and Darnell M. Whitt, *Détente Diplomacy: United States and European Security in the 1970s* (Dunellen, University Press of Cambridge, 1970), Chap. 3.

38. For a proposal on mutual reductions in stages, see Timothy W. Stanley, *A Conference on European Security? Problems, Prospects, and Pitfalls* (Atlantic Council of the United States, 1970), pp. 38–43.

39. This interest is shown in *United States Relations with Europe*, Hearings, especially in the statement of Representative Henry S. Reuss, p. 414.

40. For a discussion of options on the size of general purpose forces, including naval elements, see Schultze and others, *Setting National Priorities: The 1972 Budget* (Brookings Institution, 1971), Chaps. 3 and 4.

41. *White Paper 1970 on the Security of the Federal Republic of Germany and on the State of the German Federal Armed Forces* (Bonn: Press and Information Office of the German Federal Government, 1970), pp. 38 and 60.

Chapter 4

1. *Washington Post*, April 2, 1970.

2. Willy Brandt in an interview on Meet the Press, April 12, 1970.

3. Helmut Schmidt, "Germany in the Era of Negotiations," *Foreign Affairs*, Vol. 49 (October 1970), p. 44.

Chapter 5

1. Testimony of General David A. Burchinal in *U.S. Security Agreements and Commitments Abroad, Pt. 10: United States Forces in Europe*, Hearings before the Subcommittee on U.S. Security Agreements and Commitments Abroad of the Senate Committee on Foreign Relations, 91 Cong. 2 sess. (1970), Pt. 10, p. 2023. The original REDCOSTE program apparently called for considerably larger reductions. A *New York Times* article in January 1969 by William Beecher, cited in the Hearings, alleges that the goal originally was a reduction of 35,000 to 40,000 personnel and a saving of $100 million. General Burchinal's comments indicate that when the goals in the program were reexamined after the Soviet invasion of Czechoslovakia, some planned actions were either postponed or eliminated (Hearings, p. 2067).

2. *EUCOM Command Summaries, 1961–69* of the U.S. Department of Defense, in James D. Hessman, "Countdown to Crisis: U.S. Forces in Europe," *Armed Forces Journal*, July 11, 1970, p. 20.

3. Occupation and stationing cost data and arrangements are based on Horst Mendershausen, *Troop Stationing in Germany: Value and Cost*, prepared for U.S. Air Force Project RAND as RAND Memorandum 5881-PR (RAND Corporation, December 1968), and on *United States Forces in Europe*, Hearings, pp. 2100 and 2245.

4. In 1968 U.S. defense expenditures for services in Western Europe amounted to $600 million (Cora E. Shepler and Leonard C. Campbell, "United States Defense Expenditures Abroad," *Survey of Current Business*, Dec. 1969, pp. 40–47). Total U.S. expenditures in Western Europe, exclusive of expenditures by U.S. personnel, were estimated at $850 million in 1968.

5. Based on estimates supplied by the Department of the Army on Operation Reforger in *Military Construction Appropriations for 1970, Pt. 2: Department of the Air Force; Department of the Army*, Hearings before a Subcommittee of the House Committee on Appropriations, 91 Cong. 1 sess. (1969), Pt. 2, pp. 279–80. These calculations covered 28,000 men. Both costs and savings were increased proportionately to cover a 48,000-man division force, including support units. In addition, for present purposes no allowance was made for rotating the division to Europe for annual exercises, at an estimated cost of $13 million a year. Figures were increased by 10 percent to adjust for 1971 prices.

6. The estimate of balance-of-payments savings from the Reforger program is derived from the testimony of General Burchinal, *United States Forces in Europe*, Hearings, p. 2023.

7. This figure accounts for all military-related U.S. dependents in the European theater, including dependents of U.S. military forces not under the European Command. Testimony of General Burchinal, *United States Forces in Europe*, Hearings, p. 2088.

8. In comparison, the Department of Defense in 1969, 1970, and 1971 placed the cost of these forces at $14 billion in *Department of Defense Appropriations, Fiscal Year 1970, Pt. 2: Department of the Army*, Hearings before the Senate Committee on Appropriations, 90 Cong. 2 sess. (1969), Pt. 2, pp. 50–51; *United States Forces in Europe*, Hearings, pp. 2053–54; and *Military Posture*, Hearings before the House Armed Services Committee, 92 Cong. 1 sess. (1971), Pt. 1, p. 2598. One reason for the difference between the Defense Department figure and the higher estimate in the text and in Table 5-4 is that the Department of Defense makes no allowance for allocating a portion of administrative overhead and retirement pay costs to the forces for European contingencies. It is also possible that the estimated composition of these forces as shown in Table 5-4 is substantially different from Defense Department planning assumptions. Finally, the Department of Defense, in showing the same figure for three years, does not allow for increases in pay and prices.

9. *Defense Report on President Nixon's Strategy for Peace*, Statement of Secretary of Defense Melvin R. Laird before the House Armed Services Committee on Fiscal Years 1972–1976 Defense Program and 1972 Defense Budget, March 9, 1971, p. 77.

10. *Defense Report*, ibid.

11. *Wall Street Journal*, July 12, 1971.

12. The Federal Republic's armament plan for 1970–74 shows procurement requirements averaging $1.5 billion a year, according to the *White Paper 1970 on the Security of the Federal Republic of Germany and on the State of the German Federal Armed Forces* (Press and Information Office, German federal government), pp. 139–45. Armament procurements of $1.2 billion in 1969 and $1.3 billion in 1970 were programmed in the defense budgets.

13. "North Atlantic Assembly Draft Report on Burden-Sharing and the Economic Aspects of the Common Defense Effort," prepared by Senator Charles H. Percy, U.S. Rapporteur, Exhibit 1, *Congressional Record*, daily ed., July 10, 1970, p. S11066.

14. *Washington Post*, Oct. 9, 1970.

Index

173